Cousin Marriage in Arabs and Islam

MYSA ELSHEIKH

Cousin Marriage in Arabs and Islam
Copyright © 2024 by MYSA ELSHEIKH
Published by Musk Standard
www.muskstandard.com
info@muskstandard.com

All rights reserved. No part of this book may be reproduced, translated or transmitted in any form or by any means, electronic or mechanical, including photocopying, recording or by any information storage and retrieval system, without written permission from the author and/or publisher.

ISBN: 978-1-916800-02-1 paperback
ISBN: 978-1-916800-03-8 ebook

Contents

Introduction	1
Chapter 1 The Quran and Sunnah	17
Chapter 2 Chastity	31
Chapter 3 Knowledge of God	37
Chapter 4 Heterosexuality	45
Chapter 5 Innocent Children	55
Chapter 6 The Sane Mind	71
Chapter 7 Honour	75
Chapter 8 Just Marriage	77
Chapter 9 Preservation of Bloodlines	81
Chapter 10 The Spirit	83
Chapter 11 Identity	87
Chapter 12 Ownership	93
Chapter 13 A Real Marriage	97
Chapter 14 Humanity	99
Chapter 15 The Nature of the Genitalia	101
Chapter 16 The Best Sex	107
Chapter 17 Truth	113
Chapter 18 Family Bond	115
Chapter 19 Safety	119
Chapter 20 Afterlife	123
Chapter 21 Legitimacy of the Child	125
Chapter 22 Eternal Love	127
Chapter 23 Soulmates	129
Chapter 24 Convenience	131

Chapter 25 Independence	133
Chapter 26 Beautiful Wedding	135
Chapter 27 Knowledge of Death	139
Chapter 28 Knowledge of Family	143
Chapter 29 Preserving Richness in Family	145
Chapter 30 Self-Love	147
Chapter 31 Prevent War	149
Chapter 32 Mercy	151
Chapter 33 Family Business	153
Chapter 34 Pride	155
Chapter 35 Culture	157
Chapter 36 Love	159
Chapter 37 Shame	161
Chapter 38 Strengthen Family Ties	163
Chapter 39 Mutual Family Interests	165
Chapter 40 Better the Devil You Know	167
Chapter 41 Surname	169
Chapter 42 Music and Film	171
Chapter 43 Fashion	173
Chapter 44 Disgust	175
Chapter 45 Power	177
Chapter 46 Beauty	179
Chapter 47 Respect Mecca and Yemen	181
Chapter 48 Prevent Fornication and Adultery	183
Chapter 49 Respect Women and Men	185
Chapter 50 A Good Ending	187
About the Author	189

Introduction

The importance of a good marriage is well known. When you find a supportive partner, you become a respected elder in society, have a lawful sexual relationship and raise legitimate children. Married couples tend to live longer, have more financial stability, and enjoy a confirmed relationship built on commitment. They experience less stress and are no longer lonely, and they also gain a new family through their in-laws, as exemplified by the Prophet Mohammed (peace be upon him). However, some people view marriage as a luxury when it is very basic and can be argued to be even a human right. Everybody has a right to produce children to survive them, which is the basis for the human right to marriage. However, the most important reason for marriage is to know God. Marriage and sex give clues to the existence of God, and the Quran and Hadith say sex and marriage are signs of God.

There are different marriage traditions around the world, each giving pride to their racial identity and agenda. They are:

1. The ancient Egyptians in Africa married brother to sister to inherit the body. In this way, they preserved the body, which is essential

in African understanding of the importance of life where the body's needs are critical. These are needs such as food, drink and protection from injury.

2. Persians married maternal uncle to niece. Persians are about order and prediction, such as dreams. Therefore, the mother is seen as a weakness, such as gentle symbols in a dream, and her brother's strength, so it is as if the dream became true.

3. Caucasians marry strangers who they become familiar with first and people compatible with or what they call to be from their "league". This is because they are white, the colour of purity, and so consider their blonde children will find ideas of purity even if born from strangers. Caucasian Royals of Europe in the past married uncles and cousins, and so, likewise, many commoners, it would seem. Darwin, the biologist, was married to his cousin and, likewise, the intelligent Jewish physicist Albert Einstein. He, too, married his cousin.

4. Asians, such as Chinese, get married through matchmaking and look for those with similar personalities. In this way, there were less likely disagreements between the couples; since the Chinese are people correcting wrongs, they are not expected to make them, so they looked for what would make the couple agreeable.

5. Arabs married paternal cousins. Arabs are a race who live in the harsh, dangerous desert and so have to be careful, responsible and mindful, so they see themselves as being sane and intelligent. The paternal cousin is from the father's brother, from ideas of further of the bother, and so support safety, which is important in the survival of the Arabs in the desert.

6. Indian subcontinent, such as Pakistanis, are said to prefer to be married to paternal aunts' children. This is because they are a race

that find rest, comfort and leisure important, and the paternal aunt is the sister of the father, meaning that even if they find strength represented by the father, they still consider their tiredness represented by the aunt.

In Islam, sex outside of marriage is severely forbidden and punished, even with death. This means that any advances or suggestions, such as flirting or nakedness in public, are completely prohibited. For this reason, Muslim women cover up. They cover their hair and chest and make sure their clothes are not tight to reveal their body shape. This is commanded in the Quran. God says women are not allowed to show their beauty "except to their husbands," and they are only allowed to uncover in front of their close family, such as brothers or fathers. This means God commanded women to cover so that any sexual behaviour or images of the women are seen by the husband alone. This is a form of chastity and honour that leaves society sex-free, making it child-friendly. The society also has elderly, religious scholars and people who are offended by sexual images and nakedness and covering is a polite manner towards these categories of people. God is pure and can see His creation, so Muslims cover to respect God.

Marriages in late life are a modern thing. They argue it is because the person will be mature enough to handle the responsibility. Still, it is also practical to find a random stranger you love or even like, which is a matter many argue as fate. However, when people are certain of the merit and correctness of cousin marriage, marriage can be conducted at a young age due to the availability of the partner. People in the past married young, and in Islam, marriage is lawful with the onset of puberty, regardless of age. The Prophet Muhammed (peace be upon him) married his cousin Aisha after she reached puberty when she was only nine years old. When historically no one argued against this fact, in modern times, it is taken to extreme attacks against the holy Prophet, such as accusations of even paedophilia. This book will explain how wrong they are and that it is the opposite that Prophet Muhammed (peace be upon him) and the Quran, in their strict command to cousin marriage, historically stopped paedophilia, which is historically associated with the marriage of strangers.

Prophet Muhammed (peace be upon him) and Lady Aisha's marriage was full of wisdom. Firstly, people in the past believed that virgins were unsafe in the world since they held no strong belief in death, and therefore, they were made to remain at home. Then, when the girl marries, and her hymen is destroyed, this becomes a warning that her whole body can be destroyed. Since it warns of death, it is considered that the earlier people get married, the better. The couple have to be cousins and related in blood for the wisdom to deflower the hymen to hold true advice about death since it gives proof for one's own flesh only.

For this reason, it is the case that God made it lawful for the Prophet to fight the disbelievers in war around the time of his marriage to the virgin Lady Aisha (raa) since the Prophet Muhammed (pbuh) then became certain of the existence of death, and could therefore defend himself well in war. It is very irresponsible to think young girls like Lady Aisha would be left without knowledge of death in the dangerous desert of Arabia. They preferred to marry them young so they could be careful to save their life.

The second reason is that in Hanif (purity) belief, they believe the human face to contain an interrupted act of sex, that the nose is long and protruding like the male penis, and the mouth is empty and internal like the female vagina. They are separated in the place where the moustache grows in males. This stopped the act of sex. The face is purity and is evidence of the existence of a pure creator, God. God says in the Quran, "**Their sign is in their face.**" (48:29). They thus considered marriage as a way to know the nature of humans and the way people were created, and more so to know God. The Prophet Muhammed (pbuh) said "**in the act of sex there is *sadaga*"** (Muslim) and the word *sadaga* means charity but also means truthfulness. That the act of sex in knowing the male and female and their joining is a mirroring of the human face, and so it supports the existence of God and gives truth to people. Muslims are commanded by God, during the five daily prayers, to bow by lowering their face to waist level and then to place their face on the ground in prostration to show respect to God, the creator of the pure face.

The third reason people married early, especially Arabs, is because, like Prophet Muhammed (pbuh), Lady Aisha (as) was also born from a cousin marriage. Her parents are similar, and she has no idea about the existence of the different male and female genders or their joining in sex, and so is deeply curious about the existence of the other gender and sex, so they were married young to satisfy their strong sexual desire and to settle their curiosity. This is because they considered sexual desire as painful and harmful and leaving it without marriage is suffering. So, they married off their children as soon as they reached puberty, as was the case of Lady Aisha (raa). Prophet Muhammed (pbuh), who the Quran says was sent as a mercy to the world, would undoubtedly marry his cousin wife as soon as she reached the age of sex in their time, which is puberty, as part of his extending his mercy to his family. Prophet Muhammed (peace be upon him) said, "**The best of you are those best to their** family, and I am your best; my best will be for my family." (Ibn Maja).

In Islam, leaving marriage, sex and children for worship, such as becoming a nun or monk, is not allowed. Still, nowadays, Arabs and Muslims leave them for education and work, with marriage in late years becoming common in the Middle East. In many instances where girls are proposed marriage, they say they want to "study" instead and pursue a career. This way, they are refusing their cousins.

Despite the historical acceptance of cousin marriage around the world, especially among Arabs and Muslims, some people nowadays believe modern life is incompatible with old traditions. However, some virtues are universal, such as trust, kindness, and cousin marriage. However, still, some want to copy Western modern life, as a way of being fans of Caucasians, and see developed countries as being superior and must be copied in everything, including how they marry, as a way of bringing similar development in their poor developing countries. This is expressed in the bride wearing a white wedding gown and the groom wearing a suit, dancing slowly and embracing while listening to English music. They believe copying Western culture gives them pride and makes them superior to those who accept and practice Middle Eastern traditions.

The most important reason why some people are against cousin marriage is because they say it causes genetic diseases. The risk of cousins passing down a genetic disease is 4-7%, whilst the risk of passing down a genetic disease for the general population is 3-4%, so it's not a big difference to warrant an alarm and cause people to stop cousin marriages altogether. Of course, people undergo genetic testing before marriage. In cases where a genetic disease is identified, they can marry other cousins, distant relatives, or even strangers.

It is relevant to mention that genetic diseases are rare, few in hundreds of thousands or millions. And for a man who carries a genetic disease, his problem does not end by marrying a stranger. This is especially true when his disease is dominant in his genes, but genetic testing does help to identify solutions. Some people get hit by cars, but that doesn't stop people from driving cars. There is a greater risk of genetic diseases, such as Down Syndrome, with maternal age. The question becomes, do we stop older people from getting married and having kids? If cousin marriage were dangerous, religions throughout history would have commanded it to stop it, but it's the opposite. Abraham (to him peace) married his first cousin and so did many Jewish prophets.

Some people misunderstand that cousin marriage leads to genetic disease, which means it created them when they are absent, but the truth is that there is a slightly higher risk of passing what already exists in the genes. Saying stranger marriage children don't get diseases is to say they are cursed and not normal. It is like saying don't help them, they don't get problems. Genetic disease science is new in humanity, so there is not much on it yet to give confident facts. Sometimes, people interpret diseases with beauty; for example, a squint is seen as a sign of chastity, that they look away from the opposite sex.

Marriage to strangers usually has the story of how they met, and people especially want to do fairy tale plots of extrapolated differences so that they have an entertaining love story to their relationship to share with people.

Historically, 80% of humanity came from cousin marriages. Today, 10% of humanity—about 750 million people—are in a cousin marriage. It is believed that 50% of Muslims marry cousins, and 96% of children from cousin marriages are healthy and normal.

Modern Arabs casually insult cousin marriage with rhyming slogans such as "*alagarib agarib*", meaning "close family cause harm like scorpions." They also try to talk those interested in cousin marriage out of their marriage. When in the past, if an Arab man refused to marry his cousin, his family would kill him as they considered him shameful and wanted to spread disbelief, mischief and immoralities. Those who married strangers were considered eloped and were labelled as perverted, rare, wicked, illness, crime, and sinful. Simply put, a stranger's marriage was considered strange.

Marrying strangers is new to humanity, especially Arabs and Muslims. It is a social experiment. Unstable politics and wars in the Middle East all meant there was a movement away from old Arab traditions and Islam, and one thing is how marriages are conducted has changed to be more stranger marriages that are encouraged, accepted and praised.

The idea of giving merit to cousin marriage could be argued to exist even in English. The word "cousin" in English is possibly from "co is in"; co is in something together or joint, so it could mean a couple. This means the total meaning of a cousin is those who you couple with and marry. Sum meaning together is similar to "same", such as coming together of cousins who are alike. Skin in English could be from "is kin", meaning for family. Sex is described in the Quran as "touch", so in the English language, they recognise the touch of the skin, and therefore, sex should be in the family, such as with a cousin. A central idea in cousin marriage is that it is the relationship of the uncle's child. The uncle is from the words "un kill", meaning not give death but life; it's the relation of sex and marriage and the giving of life to a born child. The uncle is called this because he is the father's brother; words further bother, which is a state of safety that ensures life.

What is interesting is Jesus (to him peace) in the Quran is said to be from Joachim (Imran), a name which in Arabic means finding the uncle important, and Jesus (to him peace) says the Quran raised the dead, so he literally "un killed" and gave life. Prince William of Wales took Kate Middleton to Kenya, Africa, to propose, possibly because Kenya sounds like "kin yeah", and this is enough for them to marry instead of his real first cousin, Princess Beatrice. It would have been well accepted in Britain, considering that Queen Elizabeth II was a cousin to Prince Philip, her husband, and they are considered respectable, serious and loved by people worldwide. The royal Prince William marrying a commoner, Kate Middleton, is called a fairytale, not human nature, history or tradition. However, this is very dangerous. They are human, not fairies, and so shouldn't do fairytales. The royals' main work is to make their people famous as good humans, so practising fairytale marriage goes against their royal work.

The reasons for marrying strangers in modern Arabs and Muslims include:

1. They want to know the truth of the humanity of each other because they belong to different races, and they want to see them eat, drink, sleep, use the toilet and have children. They claim the Quran says, "**God created humans in tribes and races to come to know each other, and the best people are the most pious and religious.**" (49:13). They interpret this verse that God supports and commands interracial marriages. However, interracial marriages in traditional Islamic literature were considered unacceptable;

one reason is they are like a mini genocide, as the child loses full belonging to a certain tribe or race.
2. They are both Muslims and want to use the fame of weddings to make Islam famous. Claiming God says "**those who respect the symbols of God**" (22:32). Islam was spread as the Quran commands using kind advice and sound arguments.
3. They have riches and want others to witness and enjoy also, claiming God says, "**Make famous the riches of God he blessed you with." (93:11).** The Prophet Muhammed (pbuh) said that family is most worthy of gifts, and the Quran mentions giving to family.
4. Use the happiness of the wedding to correct old enmity, claiming that God says, "**They were enemies, and God befriended between their hearts**" (3:103) and "**act with enemies as if they are close friends**" (41:34). Marriage creates children who grow up in the tension and stress of feuding groups; it is not mercy.
5. A common reason for rejecting and refusing cousins is a lack of sexual attraction, as they see themselves as brothers or sisters. The Quran says, "**Call them to their real fathers, that is more just to God.**" (33:5), so they are not real brothers or sisters; it is only polite to call them that. Prophet Muhammed (pbuh) married his daughter Lady Fatimah (raa) to his cousin Ali (raa) when Ali lived with them for a long time as he was raised by Prophet Muhammed (pbuh) because his family were poor.
6. They fear that marrying their cousin and divorcing will separate and split the family permanently. The Prophet Muhammed (pbuh) said that a sign of hypocrisy is if they dispute they exaggerate in revenge (Dawud); for the whole family to get involved and separate if a couple divorces is just too extreme.

7. Terrorists claim they want to destroy disbelievers and decrease their numbers. Claiming that God says "**to marry chaste woman from the Christians and Jews**" (5:5). There are other verses that say don't marry non-Muslims until they believe and enter Islam.

Traditionally, stranger marriage is considered wrong because:

1. Love is personal and discriminative. Why love one? Why not all? Everybody else is belittled and rejected; it's like backbiting.
2. Rejecting cousin is breaking family bonds.
3. Claiming to own and take the blood and flesh of different tribes or races for their own benefit is like slavery and kills them and is genocide initiation.
4. Stranger marriages introduce children to sex by explaining different meetings (a description of sex), which is a form of paedophilia.
5. A commoner becoming royal increases the value of something unchanged. This makes it like monetary interest or usury.
6. Accepting the dirty genitalia of strangers is not the best mental health state. It is like being intoxicated with drugs and alcohol.
7. A strange woman carries the idea of harm, and so she is like an anus, making it a form of homosexuality.
8. Accepting a person whose social status is less is humiliation, and accepting inferiority is like eating a pig.
9. Sex with strangers is fornication, which in Arabs is seen as ruining plans of genealogy.
10. To take a person and their goods from another tribe or race without permission of their king or tribal elders is stealing and kidnapping.
11. Random choosing of people to marry is like chance and gambling.

12. Strangers acting as a family is like the ropes and sticks appearing like snakes; it is magic.
13. Refusing the cousin who is lawful is *Zihar* (forbidding what is allowed by God).
14. Destroying the identity of a tribe or race by reducing it in the children for your benefit is racism and genocide.
15. Doing a wedding with a stranger in a ceremony designed for cousin marriage, such as the Sudanese Jirtig, which includes the bride wearing red to symbolise blood relation with the groom, is a lie, and for guests to accept it is a false witness.
16. Strangers benefiting from family riches instead of cousins are not giving inheritances to rightful owners.
17. A man who marries a stranger so that his cousin is then forced to marry a stranger, too, is Dayouth, meaning a man of no shame.
18. Refusing cousin marriage, which the father and forefathers approved and commanded, is Egug Walidain, which means dishonouring parents.
19. Marrying strangers means old forefathers are not born again because the blood of the stranger spoils the bloodline, so it is like murder.
20. The marriage of strangers is a mixing of different, so it's an impure creation that doesn't prove a pure creator (God), so it is atheism.

It seems that to marry strangers, when it comes to making so many sinful ideas, is just someone who wants to guarantee themselves hellfire.

Having children is the greatest proof of kindness as it gives life and continues humanity, so it is a sign of mercy, especially caring for weak children. In Arabs in the desert, family life is important in showing kindness between people. Being infertile is disappointing to those who wish to prove this and is unfortunately considered a sign a person is dangerous. God says in the Quran he makes who he wishes to be infertile. Early marriages are, for this reason, important as some people give birth after a long time and so need opportunity. In traditional Arab law, giving birth and being survived is a human right.

In a time when children of cousin marriage are insulted as inbred, and that cousin relation is belittled as disgusting. This book gives the perspective of cousin marriage as a positive advantage and that profound reasons exist for them, including knowledge of God.

In some religions, cousin marriage is forbidden, such as Sidiqiya, the religion of Muslimah, the Liar. This false Arab prophet is found in mid-Arabia, which is the root of modern Wahabi Islam. In Wahabi Saudi Arabia, ruled by Al Saud, who descended from the tribe of Hanif, the same tribe as Muslimah the Liar, they have offices where the government allows strangers to marry foreigners. However, Wahabi/Salafi Muslims are a minority among Muslims. The word "Saud" in Al Saud, the royals of Saudi Arabia, means happy or very glad, such as being gay.

In some states in America, cousin marriage is illegal, so it is best to consult lawyers before practising cousin marriage in or travelling to America.

Modernly, Arabs call strangers uncles and female strangers aunts to legalise marrying their children. God says call them to their true fathers. God says, "**Words said but hold not true authority with God.**" (53:23). Pig slaughtered in the Islamic way by saying "God is great" is by no means lawful (halal). Likewise, a person of foreign blood and flesh doesn't become lawful to marry because they choose to call them family or they perform the Islamic rituals of marriage.

13

In Arabic and Islamic countries nowadays, they are curious to know what a girl's fate is and her sexual preferences, so they don't marry her to a cousin but somehow marry a suitable stranger.

Modern Arabs want to know what a girl will fetch in the market and how lucky she is based on getting a good husband. They are obsessed with slavery, where people are judged, and values are estimated based on their good characteristics. Parents and society are entertained by who would end up marrying a girl or a boy. It is random, like gambling and glorified slavery, trying to know what kind of wedding and life a stranger husband will give a girl. In Sudan, girls are said to be in the market, and unmarried girls are called *Bayra*, meaning rejected and unwanted and with low prices. When they say cousin marriage is an old tradition, they mean like an old cloth faded, ripped, torn and stinks. They believe marrying strangers is sophisticated and civilised. God says in the Quran, "**the Devil beautifies to them their sins**" (8:48).

In a stranger marriage, a girl is supposed to attract a mate, so they resort to wearing make-up, radiating perfume, no hijab, free mixing, and even accepting flirting. Parents usually arrange cousin marriage as they recognise the importance of marriage for their kids. Modern Arabs have memorised phrases such as marriage is "*gisma and naseeb*" (share of fate and luck), and when told the Quran command for cousin marriage, they say it is meant for Prophet Muhammed (pbuh) only, and the rest of Muslims should marry as they wish.

Wars in Europe, such as World War One and Two, have caused changes in culture; the once fully covered women of Europe wore little since there was less fabric for clothes and so nakedness. Arab and Muslim cultures became influenced by copying what they see in the Western media. Those who marry strangers are difficult to convince

Introduction

of cousin marriage, they don't listen, and it is as if they are bewitched. This is strange since, historically, stories of cousin love and marriage, including Abella and Anter and Gais and Leila, are the gold standard of romance in Arabs and Islam. Strangers who were lovers were seen as socially unacceptable and had to elope to the outskirts of town.

Recognising the merits of cousin marriage, discussed in this book in at least fifty chapters and explained in a different chapter, parents should arrange cousin marriage for their children but not force it; they should act as matchmakers. The Quran says there should be no compulsion in religion, let alone in marriage, regardless of perceived merit.

This book is an invitation to think about human marriage choices and the best choices and reasons behind them.

> Cousin marriage is pure as both are the same
> But stranger's love is untrue to them it's a game.
> When God and religion are your aim
> You think and analyse how humans came
> So you choose a cousin who shares blood and a name
> And disregard those with genetic disease claim
> For a stranger marriage is just a shame
> This is to avoid the hellfire with heat and flame

Chapter I

The Quran and Sunnah

Muslims believe the Quran is the literal words of God, and the Sunnah as the sayings and deeds of Prophet Muhammed (pbuh). Together, the Quran and Sunnah make up the religion of Islam. Anything mentioned in them is seen as important and obligatory worship in Islam. Cousin marriage is mentioned by name in the Quran and Sunnah. This explicitness can be understood because of how important it is to God and Islam.

The Quran says, "**God has made legitimate the Prophet's wives who he paid their dowry and the slave girls who God gave him, and likewise the daughters of his paternal uncles and the daughters of his paternal aunts, and the daughters of his maternal uncles and daughters of his maternal aunts, with preference to those who migrated with him to Medina. Lawful is a believing woman who gives herself to the prophet in times of hardship, if the prophet wants** to wed her to be exclusive for him alone without other believing men. God knows what He has made obligatory to the believers in their marriage and the wedding of their slaves, as to be no shame against the believers and God is forgiving and merciful." (Quran 33:50). This verse explains four categories of cousins, mentioned in order of priority. This listing is traditionally understood as if they can't find a first cousin, marry a second cousin, etc., always to look at the family, tribe and person's own race. Searching for compatibles who are similar to them. These groups of girls a man may select a wife from are called his *Majaweez.*

The Quran gives preference to the paternal cousin over the maternal cousin. This is because men prefer women less than their mothers. All women came from men, and men find better women from their own men such as uncle, than women from strangers, as it is just pure. Straight men don't want women associated with strange men. Men should consider a paternal uncle's daughter, then a paternal aunt, then the daughter of the maternal uncle and then the daughter of the maternal aunt, et cetera. Cousins have degrees of purity, and paternal cousins are purer and better than maternal cousins. Because God in Islam is completely pure, Muslims marrying should choose the best relationship and purest.

Some have interpreted this verse as allowing cousin marriage, but as God says, "obligatory" makes it a command to perform. The verse also allows a man to marry his slave, and there is compassion to marry a stranger to elevate her hardship, what is called *"Heba."*

Heba marriage is for royals, prophets, the rich and pious, and anyone with the means to help a stranger—those who can afford to treat needy women with respect. The man's status is proof that it's a marriage seeking good. The man needs to be married to his cousin first to help the family. Islam appreciates meaning; for example, there are different rulings for accidental vs intentional killing. God is Mugsit, meaning one who appreciates intentions and meanings. *Heba* is a humanitarian case, but this was rare; royals, rich people, or scholars are usually trusted to be good to poor women. Extenuating circumstances include when there's no cousin or because they're in a distant land or at war; they can then marry strangers because there is compassion in the religion of Islam. In fact, the Damsel in distress is a fantasy of many men, which is mercy for women who are in this situation.

An example of *heba* marriage, is the marriage of prophet Moses, from the girl he found near the well waiting to give her animals water to drink.

As well as the explicit mention of cousin marriage in the verse above, there are other mentions of cousin marriage in the Quran, primarily implicit. For instance, God says about a woman married to her cousin, and they divorced and want to return to each other, but her family refused, that they should remarry since it's "**purer and more chaste.**" (2:232).

The Quran also prohibits stranger marriages; God says, "**It is not legitimate to marry from the general women after this, even if be a replacement of a wife or he is pleased by her beauty, except for women who are slaves. And God is watchful of all things**" (33:52). The Quran says even if a stranger is very beautiful still not allowed since beauty is not necessarily feminine since men can be handsome like Joseph who is mentioned in the Quran. In Sudanese Arabic, female genitalia is called "Jamal", "what makes her beautiful", as all other parts of the body can be similar to men except for the genitalia; it's the place of true difference of genders, and so is the main site of pleasure and beauty. Some believe the wedding ceremony can make strangers' marriages valid; saying the correct prayers can not make a pilgrimage to Paris a valid Hajj.

Prophet Muhammed (pbuh) says in the Hadith, **"The end of the world would not come until men leave their cousin without even looking at them and marrying instead strangers."** (Haithami). He (pbuh) also said explicitly, **"The best horse is the black horse and the best wife is the paternal cousin"** (Ibn Al Gaisrani).

Prophet Muhammed (pbuh) said, **"Love of the Arabs is a sign of belief in Islam"** (Iraqi). This does not only mean loving the Arabs but also what Arabs prefer in love, which is cousin marriage. Arabs are a race that wants to survive the harm of the desert, and believers want to avoid the harm of God's eternal hellfire, so this similarity creates love.

The Quran says Moses pulled Aaron's hair. Hair represents a child (in English, heir is similar to hair); as hair has no feeling, a child can't feel a parent in marriage. Moses pulling Aaron's hair means he will take his son, meaning a cousin marriage.

One common argument against cousin marriage is that there is a Hadith that says, "Don't marry close relatives because children are then born weak". This has no evidence to be from Prophet Muhammed (pbuh), and even if it did, it would be interpreted as forbidding close relatives like mother, sister, daughter, niece, aunt and grandmother, who the Quran explicitly forbids men not to marry. In Islam, marriage, it is also prohibited to marry wet nurses and children he was breastfed with.

The descendants of Prophet Muhammed's (pbuh) family and descendants are called "ashraf" (honourable), and they were known to marry cousins and relatives in their history.

Prophet Muhammed (pbuh) tells a story about men who went into a cave, and then a large rock fell in the opening, and each man prayed to God, mentioning the good deeds they did. One man says he was going to fornicate with his cousin and even sat on top of her but then remembered God, so he stopped and did not have sex with her, and when he prayed to God using this deed as proof of his sincerity, the rock moved. This shows that the Prophet agreed that sex and marriage should be between cousins.

In Islam, as mentioned in the chapter of the Light of the Quran, a person is only allowed to eat uninvited at the homes of certain relatives, so then how can the marriage of strangers be allowed in Islam? People don't knock on random strangers' doors to eat dinner with them uninvited, so then it's difficult to accept asking for sex and marriage from strangers.

As for the deeds of Prophet Muhammed (pbuh), the Prophet's parents were cousins, all his wives were first or distant cousins and all his daughters married cousins. The companions of Prophet Muhammed (pbuh) were also from cousin marriages, such as Ali (raa), his cousin, whose parents were first cousins.

Prophet Mohammed's (peace be upon him) father was Abdullah, son of Abdul Mutalab (1st grandfather), son of Hashim (2nd grandfather), son of Abdu Manaf (3rd grandfather), son of Gussai (4th grandfather), son of Kilab (5th grandfather), son of Murrah (6th grandfather). Prophet Mohammed's mother was Amina, daughter of Wahab, son of Abdu Manaf (1st grandfather), son of Zahra (2nd grandfather), son of Kilab (3rd grandfather), son of Murrah (4th grandfather). Mohammed's parents were cousins. They meet in his father's fifth and mother's third grandparent, Kilab the son of Murrah. Amina, the Prophet's mother, was born into a cousin's marriage, and his father, Abdullah, was also born into a cousin's marriage. Prophet Muhammed (pbuh) said in a Hadith that all his ancestors were born into marriages like those of Islam. This means cousin marriage is the marriage of Islam.

Prophet Muhammad's (peace be upon him) parents were not first cousins, but their grandfathers were. This, as well as his wives, were not first cousins except for one; they related to him in their great grandfathers, who were paternal first cousins. This is mercy and compassion as it shows persistence in marrying a cousin even if the first cousin is not available. Some people wrongfully marry strangers if they don't have a first cousin without looking further into their relatives. Prophet Muhammed (pbuh) is more blessed due to the meaning of numbers in parent relations because cousin marriage meaning is important in life, even when cousins from far grandfathers still count.

The wives of Prophet Muhammad (pbuh) were also all his cousins and related to him in his forefathers:

1. Khadija, daughter of Khuwaild, was his cousin, and they met in her 3rd and his 4th grandfather (Gussai)
2. Um Habiba Ramlah, daughter of Abu Sufyan, was his cousin, and they met in her 4th and his 3rd grandfather (Abdu Manaf)
3. Um Salama Hind, daughter of Umyah, was his cousin, and they met in her 5th and his 5th grandfather (Kilab), the same grandfather Prophet Muhammed's parents met in the bloodline.
4. Aisha, daughter of Abu Baker, was his cousin, and they met in her 7th and his 6th grandfather (Murrah). She was the only virgin wife. Her ancestor was Taim, son of Murrah, and his name in Arabic sounds like "perfect woman". Arabs believe cousin is a complete female as strangers have ideas of harm, making them like an anus.

5. Hausa, daughter of Omar the son of Khattab, was his cousin, and they met in her 9th and his 8th grandfather (Luay).
6. Sauda, daughter of Zuma, was his cousin, and they met in her 8th and his 8th grandfather (Luay).
7. Zainab, daughter of Jahsh, was his cousin, and they met in her 9th and his 14th grandfather (Khuzymah). She was also his first cousin from his paternal aunt Umaima.
8. Jewairiyah, daughter of Harith, was his cousin, and they met in her 11th and his 16th grandfather (Alyas)
9. Maymoona, daughter of Harith, was his cousin, and they met in her 16th and his 17th grandfather (Mudar)
10. Zainab, daughter of Khuzymah. She was his cousin, and they met in her 15th and his 17th grandfather (Mudar)
11. Safiyah daughter of Huyay. A Jewish princess who became a prisoner of war, she met with Prophet Muhammed (pbuh) in their mutual ancestor, Prophet Abraham.

Prophet Mohammed (pbuh) before Islam proposed to his paternal first cousin, Um Hani Fakhita, daughter of Abu Talib, son of Abdul Mutalab, Ali's 4th caliph of Islam sister. Unfortunately, her father refused the proposal and gave her to a man from their tribe, Quraish. When the Prophet (peace be upon him) confronted him, his uncle said the man was in-laws, and he wanted to be generous to them. After Islam, Um Hani divorced, and Prophet Mohammed (pbuh) proposed marriage again to his cousin, but she refused, saying she had the responsibility to care for her kids. The Prophet Muhammed (pbuh) commented that "**the best Arab women are from the tribe of Quraish, for they are kind to kids and protective of husband belonging**" (Haithami). The Prophet (pbuh), even if he had married his first cousin Fakhita, would have married and loved Aisha more since their relationship is similar to that between his parents and so something similar to his understanding and nature.

The Prophet's paternal first cousin, Umama, daughter of Hamza and son of Abdul Mutalib, was presented to him in marriage. He said she was his brother's daughter, as he and her father, Hamza, were breastfed by the same woman (Bukhari).

As for Prophet Muhammed's (pbuh) daughters' marriage, they are all married cousins.

1. Fatimah (raa) married her father's paternal first cousin Ali (raa).
2. Um Kalthoom married her father's paternal first cousin Utayba son of Abu Lahab.
3. Rugaya married her father's paternal first cousin Utba, son of Abu Lahab.
4. Zaineb married Alass son of Rabiah's, who was her maternal cousin. His mother was Halah, daughter of Khuwailid, and her mother was Khadijah daughter of Khuwailid.

Um Kalthoom and Rugaya, after divorcing their husbands due to their father Abu Lahab's severe hatred of Islam, married Othman, Son of Afan. Uthman's 4th grandfather was Manaf who is Prophet Muhammed (pbuh) 3rd grandfather, and Uthman's mother was a cousin of Prophet Muhammed (pbuh). His maternal grandmother was the paternal aunt of Prophet Muhammed (pbuh). Uthman himself his parents were cousins, meeting in their 3rd grandfather. Both parents were from a man called Abd Shams.

Utayba, after the chapter of Massad of the Quran was revealed, it said his father Abu Lahab was going to enter hellfire. He came to Prophet Muhammed (pbuh) and claimed he was a disbeliever, then made a display, then spitted and divorced Um Kalthoom. The Prophet Muhammad (peace be upon him) cursed him and said may God oppress him with a dog from God's dogs, and he was eaten by a lion. Perhaps this story is the basis for killing those who refuse cousin marriage in Arabs and Islam.

Omar, son of Khatab, the second Caliph in Islam, had parents who were cousins; they met a grandfather called Kaab. His mother and his father met in their eighth grandfather. His first wife was from his clan of Makhzoom. After embracing Islam, Omar married Atika, the daughter of Zaid son of Amru son of Nafil. He and her father were first cousins. The name "Umar" is from "am ar" meaning "of the view of marrying from paternal cousin".

The Prophet's companion Urwa, son of Masoud Althgafi, son Dawud, married his maternal cousin, despite wars and migration and the fact that Muslims weren't allowed to marry their cousins if they were disbelievers. Prophet Muhammed (pbuh) said this companion's face looked most like that of Prophet Jesus, son of Mary.

Differences in characteristics between married men and women can expose and emphasise differences in genitalia. Prophet Muhammed (pbuh) commanded, "**marry compatible women and marry your daughters to compatible men**" (Al Shawkani). God says in the Quran that He was not born, nor did he give birth and added, "**There are none compatible with God**" (112). The devil's name in Arabic is Iblees from the words "ab la sawa" (parents not same), and therefore, his main work is whispering to get strangers to marry to make many sins in this one act. Marriage of strangers has ideas of impurity and emphasises differences such as the genitalia.

Like the devil, the jinn is created from fire and fires is made from joining and rubbing different things.

Some Muslims interpret the Hadith, "**Whoever comes with pleasing religion and character, marry them to your daughters,**" as meaning marry strangers as long as they are religious and polite. This Hadith means compatibility that a man and woman must have similar and pleasing religion and character.

Compatibility in Islam is in ten things:

1. In genealogy, both should be cousins from the same tribe and race. God says in the Quran, "**from among God's signs is suitable marriage partners who are from their own people.**" (30:21). All four schools of thought in Sunni Islam speak of *kafa* (compatibility in genealogy), such as saying Arabs should marry Arabs, etc.
2. The marrying couple should be male and female. Prophet Muhammed (pbuh) said, "**Women are the other half of men.**" (Abu Dawud). God in the Quran forbids homosexuality by admonishing those men who "**have sex with other men with desire instead of women.**" (7:81).
3. Compatibility in the body, such as age and circumcision. Prophet Muhammed (pbuh) said, "**If the two circumcised genitalia meet, then they should take a purity bath.**" (Ibn Rajab). Circumcision is a beauty and prepares and permits sexual intercourse and pleasure. Babies are born with skin covering the sensitive part of their genitalia. Boys have the penis glans covered, while girls have the clitoris covered. These coverings are pure so that the baby is not said to have had sex with the mother during birth since the sensitive parts are covered by skin. Sex with parents is great impurity; a parent's purity suggests God's purity. Circumcision

is removing these skins to prepare for marriage. Also, the couple should be on the same level of beauty, and cousins should marry those who look similar, such as those who are similar in height and skin colour. Prophet Muhammed (pbuh) was of average height, so not different from his wives. Lady Aisha knew that if a woman who was his cousin was beautiful, the Prophet would marry her, as he was very handsome. Aisha's mother was said to be as beautiful as the celestial virgins in paradise. Please note that circumcision, where all the female genitalia is removed, was prohibited by Prophet Muhammed (pbuh). It is called Female Genital Mutilation, and it's illegal around the world. As for age, the Quran says Prophet Zakariyah (as) said, "**But I am an old man, and my wife is menopausal.**" (3:40), when he was told he would have a boy, meaning John the Baptist (as). This shows that men should marry from their age when possible.

4. Puberty, has reached adulthood, which in Islam and Arabs starts at puberty. This means the emission of semen by males and menstruation in females. Prophet Muhammed (pbuh) said, "**marry loving and fertile women**" (Iraqi), meaning after puberty, because that is when males and females become fertile. This Hadith prohibits child marriage and paedophilia.

5. Their work and their parents' work. Moses married a girl after doing her job, and her dowry was working for her as a shepherd. Joseph refused a relationship because he was a servant, and the woman was a master's wife. The Quran divorced an aristocratic woman from her slave husband since they were different and not compatible. Prophet Muhammed (pbuh), who was a lord in his tribe of Qurish, married a Jewish woman whose family was the leader of the Jews.

6. Similar lifestyle, God says, "**with preference to those who immigrated with the Prophet.**" (33:50). Ali was raised in the Prophet's household, making him like Fatima, and they married.
7. Character such as honour. The. Quran says, "**a fornicator must marry only a fornicator or one who was before disbeliever.**" (24:3). And "**Those pure and good should marry pure and good, and the wicked should be married to the wicked.**" (24:26).
8. Dignity: a freeman marries a free woman, and an enslaved person should marry an enslaved person or one who has slave ancestry. A prince should marry a princess and not a servant. A lady married to an enslaved person was divorced by the Quran. This is because joining different is impure, and God is pure. Marriage to those less or weaker can be considered sexual abuse and should be avoided, as it is an injustice.
9. Islamic religion. The Quran says, "**Do not marry disbelievers until they believe and become Muslim.**" (2:221). In the Prophet's time, when Islam was new, some Muslim partners were not Muslim, so they separated and divorced from them. The Prophet said to marry "**one whose religion pleases**", meaning Islam.
10. Virgin to virgin and mature to mature. Prophet Muhammed (pbuh) asked a man why he did not marry a virgin (Muslim). The Quran says to marry a divorced woman to her previous husband and not a new virgin man as to be pure and chaste.

God says in the Quran, "**don't force girls into prostitution**" (24:33), meaning not forcing them to marry strangers instead of poor cousin, seeking money and riches like prostitution.

The Quran tells the story of when Prophet Muhammad's (pbuh) adopted son was considered literally as a real Prophet Muhammad's son, so he married Prophet Muhammad's cousin. Prophet Muhammad considered he was more rightful to his cousin but was ashamed to say so, but God revealed in the Quran that Zaineb was to divorce Zayed and for her to return and to marry Prophet Mohammed (peace be upon him). This story highlights how important cousin marriage is to God and His Prophet.

In Islam, it is believed that Eve, the first female human created by God and the mother of all humanity, was created from the ribs of Adam, her husband. This shows that the original design was that a wife should be related biologically to her husband, and this is understood in Islam as a cousin marriage. Adam's sons married their sisters. They were born as twins, a male and a female, and each male married a different twin. This also shows that marrying from family is valid to God.

In Islam, the Quran says no one should marry too close, like a sister or go far with strangers, but a middle, like a cousin. The Prophet Muhammed (pbuh) said, "**The best of issues is being in the middle.**" (Iraqi).

The Quran says that people will have "pure" partners in heaven. They will be happy to marry their cousins since all the rancour that separated them in this world will be removed from their hearts.

The Quran says, "**God creates people in pairs**" (78:8), meaning God creates brothers and sisters to allow their children to practice cousin marriage. Cousins are not to be "**sold separately**". They are like multipack. In forbidding strangers from marrying, God says, "**Believers are brothers**" (49:10), meaning no marriage is allowed between them. The Quran says, "**The two different rivers meet without mixing to be pure.**" (55:19-20). That differents shouldn't join, so two strangers shouldn't become one in the union.

The Quran prescribes the crucifixion of some criminals. It is a wood cross from trees, and trees represent need as they cannot move from their place to water. The cross is two lines of opposite directions to mean the meeting of different genders in sex. The total meaning of the wooden cross is purity by the absence of sex. The Quran says Jesus, born from the pure Virgin Mary, was not crucified, as it is not suitable, as he knows purity more than most people, as he was born from a virgin. God in the Quran says "**Jesus was not killed on the cross, but it was made to seem so**" (4:157), meaning there was a misunderstanding.

The Quran commands Muslims to pray to God to give them partners and children who please their eyes, and this is cousin marriage. The Quran also describes the prophets as being "**offspring who come from each other**" (3:34), meaning they were produced from cousins and relatives, such as Isaac, whose parents are Abraham and Sarah, who were cousins.

In Islam, the prayer *"ya hanan ya manan"* means that God should be "loving like family and fulfilling wishes" to believers. This means that cousins marry since semen should go to the family. This is because semen fulfils the wish of having children.

Those sexually attracted to strangers should accept that this is a false desire of the ego and whisper of the devil. People should lower their gaze on the opposite sex, females should wear the hijab, and there should be segregation of the genders in the teachings of Islam.

Good marriages based on the Quran and Sunnah are acts of worship, and bad marriages that go against the religion's teachings are sinful and could be punished in eternal hellfire.

CHAPTER 2

Chastity

The human beings release abhorrent things from their body. This includes faeces, urine, farts, pubic hair, sweat, menstrual blood, ear wax, dead skin, pus from wounds or spots, saliva, nose snot, semen, hymen blood, morning mouth smell, dandruff and vaginal excretions and odours. This makes human beings worthy of covering themselves so as not to remind of their excrement, and this is especially true of their private genitalia, which is something most people are keen to do by themselves without the need for advice. In many countries, nakedness in public is illegal and can be against the law. These common-sense rules protect society against lewdness.

Arab men and women wear long dresses to avoid clothes that have details in the middle, such as trousers or skirts, since they emphasise the genitalia. As part of preventing harm, they avoid attracting attention to the middle of their body.

These excrements make it difficult for people to want to sleep with random strangers due to the disgust from these excrements. This is perhaps the reason why God, who is pure and is the God of chastity, creates them so that people do not act like animals and randomly mate but preserve the act of sex between the married cousin couple. However, these excrements do not seem as bad when considering family, which is why cousin marriage is easier and fresher than strangers. Just like a mother doesn't feel so disgusted by the nappies of her own child. For instance, people, out of disgust, refuse to eat the leftovers of strangers in restaurants, but if a brother or cousin leaves them, they eat the leftover food without problem. Family are merciful and kind due to the relationship of the womb, which is an empty round muscle in the genitalia that means a lack of harm.

When nowadays they claim cousin marriage is disgusting, perhaps we can turn the table and say perhaps they mean people who do cousin marriage are disgusted by the genitalia of strangers. Arabs have a special word for chastity based on disgust, it is "*iffa*". *Iffa* is from word *aff* meaning feel disgust and feeling of revulsion. Health in Arabic is called "*Affiyah*", meaning "can recognise what is disgusting". Prophet Muhammed (pbuh) said people should ask God for "Affiyah" in prayer (Bukhari). Arab girls are called "Afaf" meaning pure, chaste and honourable.

Another disgusting thing in the human genitalia is the congenital skin cover over the penis glans in males and the clitoris in females. This skin prevents ideas of sex and the joining of the baby's genitalia to the mother's genitalia, which in purity are removed as children prepare for sex and marriage.

In Islam, there is a strict hygiene code, such as *Istijmar*, which is having a barrier between the person and faeces and urine so that there is no direct touch with excrement. This is like using toilet paper or, historically, in Arabs and Muslims, using pebbles. Other cleaning includes using water to wash the genitalia after using the toilet called "*Istinja*". Or by doing a body wash called *gusl* after finishing period or engaging in sexual acts. The God of Islam, Allah, is completely pure and so commands purity in the religion of Islam. This means Muslims take these disgusting elements of the human very seriously; it is the case that if Muslim farts, they require a wash called *wudu* before prayer or touching the holy Quran. Muslims such as Alrazi invented soap, all inspired by God's love for purity mentioned in the Quran. Prophet Muhammed (pbuh) said, "**Cleanliness is a sign of belief in God and religion.**" (Iraqi). In modern life, soap, shampoo, perfume and deodorant ease sex and marriage with strangers. Likewise, makeup and fashion are used to entice strangers into sex and marriage.

When strangers marry, they feel obliged to prove they really tolerate and love each other and cherish each other, as some lead them to do oral sex, leading to drinking urine, licking faeces from the anus or smelling body odour. That they accept each other's harm and accept their shortcomings. Arab men pinch women they fornicate or commit adultery with to tell them that what they are doing is wrong. Cousins are not embarrassed to be told by their spouse to be clean or put on perfume, but strangers can feel offended; it is a sensitive issue.

Cousin marriage is all about good things, and since it holds good meanings, they use good things to emphasise their love, such as perfume and incense and burning fragrant woods, such as sandalwood and oud. In Sudan, traditional Arab women married to cousins use *Dukhan* (lit. Smoking). *Dukhan*, or *Bakhour*, is a hole inside the floor, burning fragrant wood that the woman sits next to and covers the hole and body. This is to perfume her body and sweat the old skin and to be clean from the period smell and pure before sex. This is an old Arab tradition that even Prophet Muhammed (pbuh) commented on, saying, "**If a woman performs *Bakhour,* she should not come to the mosque for prayers**" (Muslim) because she becomes too sexually provocative. The Muslim Arabs of Sudan also use perfumed exfoliants called "*Dilka*" on their skins and homemade perfumes with musk, sandalwood, and some types of fragrant crocodile scales called "*Dufra*".

Prophet Muhammed (pbuh) said, "**We don't see anything as good as marriage to lovers**" (Baihagi). This is because marriage has sex which involves harmful genitalia, so some fear that sex may offend or spoil their love. Some modern people say because marriage involves genitalia that, they prefer strangers as they don't want to cause harm to their family by marrying and having sex with their cousin. Historically, Arabs had a special type of love called *Hub Uzri* (lit. Virginal love or platonic love), which is when they love strangers, so they don't get married and have no sexual consummation. In movies, pimps beat and humiliate prostitutes as a form of training to accept strangers' harmful genitalia.

Swords are symbols of cousin marriage. That a person is further from harm, which is symbolised by the sword cuts, and it's long, so it's like saying far harm. Ali, son of Abu Taleb (raa), had a sword called "*Zu Faqar*", as it emphasises the meaning of matrimony by having a split into two at the far end. It is relevant to mention that Ali's sword (raa) was a gift from his cousin Prophet Muhammed (pbuh) to replace an old, broken one.

The Quran says, "**Lord don't burden us with that we are not capable to bear**" (2:286), and this could imply cousin marriage as it's easier to accept, while strangers' genitalia can be stressful, disgusting, and depressive to accept, deal with and have sex within a marriage. The Quran also says, "**Marry those who hold good meaning with you or those who you find good and acceptable**" (4:3). People look for things to make sex easy due to the bad meaning of genitalia. Cousin marriage meanings are beautiful since it's a pure relationship. Some people find that they feel fearful, disgust, horror, sadness, and anxious feelings accompanying the idea of marrying strangers. Traditionally, accepting strangers was seen as accepting humiliation and shame. Accepting harm from strangers is humiliation, and cousin marriage, in its praiseworthy description, is dignity and pride.

In Islam, when Muslims declare their belief in God, they touch the middle finger to the thumb in a circle and raise the index finger. This is to say the middle, and they mean the genitalia, which is a little like a thumb to mean purity. The index finger is raised to mean praise of God. This teaches Muslims against impurity in strangers' marriages.

Prophet Muhammed's (pbuh) favourite meat was the shoulder, and he said it's far from ideas of harm, meaning it's far from the genitalia of the animal. Likewise, the bodies of people who want to marry must have good meanings far from ideas of harm. Prophet Muhammed's (pbuh) name means the chaste one, or pure, or honourable one.

Traditionally, girls feel shame that if she doesn't marry their cousin, then some strange girl marries her cousin, smells his farts and sees him going to the toilet, coming to know of the size of his genitalia and cleaning his baby faeces. Man worries strange man marrying cousin instead of him smelling her farts and period blood etc. This is why some people find it easier to marry their cousins. The man coming back from work sweaty and stinking, his cousin can accept, but strangers find it difficult to accept such ideas.

People who marry strangers, when asked if they are disgusted by their spouse's genitalia, say it is nothing, it is alright, and they forgive. They belittle harm. Arabs magnify harm to avoid it. Ali, son of Abu Talib, was a knight who avoided and healed harm. The Quran says Abraham was *"awab,"* which means to be frightened and shocked by harm. This is because they feared God and the hellfire.

Some claim they marry strangers as a way to normalise the genitalia and human bodily functions so that doctors aren't disgusted by the ill vomiting or diarrhoea, or civil engineers planning toilets or coach travelling stopping for the toilets in services. They wish to support the development of civilisation.

From childhood, children are raised knowing genitalia is disgusting and must be clean, and as they grow, they are taught not to accept harm from strangers. Teaching children to love the honourable descendants of Prophet Muhammed (pbuh) and the dignity of royals, teaching children about hygiene and calling them princesses or princes or heroes to make them feel special, important and dignified. The Quran says, "**God gave humans dignity**" (17:20). It also says how Adam and Eve covered their genitalia with leaves in shame after disobeying God and eating from the forbidden tree.

CHAPTER 3

Knowledge of God

Knowledge of God is very important. It is essential that everyone has access to understanding about their creator, just as they do know their parents. Just as knowing our parents gives us the resources, help and support, God is a great resource and provider of help and support. God says in the Quran, "**God who answers the prayers of those desperate for help and removes harm**" (16:62). God also requires people to know of Him and worship Him as He demands in religion. This makes knowledge of God very critical, and anything that deprives us of knowledge of God is very harmful and should be prevented. God in Islam is perfect and has absolutely no shortcomings; he is a good and merciful God, which not only makes Muslims love God but also makes knowing God the greatest pleasure a person may experience in their life.

It is the case that a child of a cousin marriage is born with the knowledge of God, and children of strangers are born without knowledge of God, which makes them born atheists. This is probably the reason why God in the Quran commands cousin marriage and prohibits marriage to strangers. God says, **"From the signs of God is that He creates for people from among their own people marriage partners"** (30:21). That a sign of God is that marriage of people from themselves, meaning from their own families and race, gives proof of God.

The child of a cousin marriage has two parents who are similar and are the same in flesh and blood, and their joining is thus a joining of similarities, so it's a pure union. This is like adding water to water; it is still pure. This purity in marriage, which is the way of creating, is thus evidence for the existence of a pure Creator, Allah, the God of Islam. This is the basis of knowledge of God for a Muslim. That God is pure since they were created from a pure creation, a joining of similarities. However, a child of strangers, their parents are of different flesh and blood, and it is a joining of different, so it's an impurity. This is like adding ink to water; it becomes impure and cannot be used to wash for prayer in Islam. This impurity in creating means there is no pure creator, no God, and so it is atheism. This means a child of strangers is born without knowledge of God and is in an impurity that doesn't leave them to appreciate the existence of a pure Creator, God.

It is the case that this is innate knowledge, and even if a child is left in the middle of the desert or the jungle and only knows their parents are cousins, they will come to appreciate the existence of a pure God. However, a child of strangers, even if born from the bloodline of Prophet Muhammed (pbuh) and having parents who are Muslim scholars, and living in a Muslim community, can come to doubt the existence of God in their creation and what they do know naturally, there is no appreciation of a pure creator, God.

This innate knowledge of God that a child is born with is called *fitrah*. Prophet Muhammed (pbuh) warned that "**a child is born Muslim, Christian or Jew based on their parents**" (Bukhari). Children born of cousin marriages find Islam easier to choose, as it advocates a pure God. In contrast, those born of strangers, who are told their creation is impure, and therefore the creator is also impure, have no difficulty accepting Christianity or Judaism. Christians believe in a God who has children, thereby associating divinity with the impurities of sex. Jews claim that God is tired and rested, which implies an impurity and shortcoming of God. In Islam, God is considered to be perfect. God says in the Quran, "**To God is the most perfect example**"(16:60). In commanding cousin marriage and prohibiting the marriage of strangers, God decreed that only children who will know His existence be born. God says, "**God only created the humans and jinn so they may worship Him**" (51:56). Thus, worshipping God is the reason for our creation, and therefore, it defeats the purpose of being born people who do not appreciate the existence of God. This means children from strangers who do not appreciate a pure God exists in their nature. Humans were made from mud, water and earth to worship God and be pure. Earth is obedient as lower with footsteps, and water is pure, so the total meaning is to follow what God gives of pure commands.

Cousin marriage is important as a sign of God. In Islam, we believe Prophet Abraham (as) tried to kill his mixed-race son Ishmael after being commanded to do this in a dream from God. The reason God commanded for him to be sacrificed was because he was not from cousin marriage and did not appreciate the existence of God. Then, when Ishmael submitted to God and acknowledged himself to be worthy of death, God accepted him and sent a sheep to be slaughtered instead of Ishmael. In Islam, all Muslims who can afford to slaughter a sheep during the Hajj period do so in recognition of the spiritual station of the prophet Ishmael. Even against the odds, Ishmael believed in God, even when everything told him to disbelieve and become an atheist, such as his birth from strangers; he instead chose God and obeyed God even if it meant his own death. This is why God honoured Ishmael by making him also a prophet, and he called people towards God. Ishmael also helped his father Abraham build the House of God in Mecca and is the ancestor to Prophet Muhammed (pbuh), the greatest Prophet God sent to people.

People are comforted by religion. God says in the Quran, **"Is it not in the mention of God people find comfort?"** (13:28). This means people are comforted by the mention and the knowledge of the good God and feel safe and comfortable with religious people, believing they will have greater character and morals. Thus, a connection to God is essential in our dealings with each other. A child of cousins who is born pure, knowing God, is bound to be a good person. In contrast, a child of strangers born into atheism who does not believe in God is, by extrapolation, bound to be bad-mannered, evil, and potentially criminal. To emphasise the idea of God and cousin marriage, Prophet Muhammed (pbuh) journeyed to the heavens on a night he was staying in his cousin Um Hani's house to gain a vision of God.

In the Middle East, where people commonly marry cousins, there is a tradition where a child takes their parents on a Hajj (greater pilgrimage) to visit the House of God in Mecca. This is because cousin parents give children a basis for belief in God, so the child wants to repay their parents by taking them on a pilgrimage to increase their parents' faith in God by witnessing the House of God.

Marriage to just any cousin doesn't support God; it has to be to the most compatible cousin to form the purest relationship since God in Islam is perfect in purity. The Quran says, "**Those who are atheist due to lack of God's signs**" (41:40). God also says, "**Who is more unjust than those who stop people from worshipping God?**" (2:114). Cousin marriage is illegal in many states in America. This is because cousin marriage is a pure relation and proves a pure God, the God of Islam. However, since they are Christians and believe in a son to God, this is impure since it associates sex and children with God. To preserve Christianity in America, they prohibited cousin marriage. It is about time these Islamophobic laws are abolished, and people should have the right and freedom to choose Islam by having children through cousin marriage.

Prophet Muhammed's (pbuh) uncle Abu Lahab was also from two tribes and was mixed race; he refused the religion of purity, the religion of Islam, and became a great enemy to Prophet Muhammed (pbuh) and Islam.

In Islam, it is obligatory for children to pray the five daily prayers from the age of seven. This shows the importance of a child's connection to God.

Muslims are not allowed to marry their father or mother as it's impure, and the parents are a symbol of God. This means if they marry parents, it insults God as being impure and doesn't exist. This includes wet nurses who breastfeed the child. Milk symbolises knowledge, so sex is supposed to give knowledge that God exists, so milk relation is considered not allowed as considered like family.

Eve, the mother of all humanity, was not created from Adam's mouth to cook for him, nor from his hand to protect his ownership; she was not created from his genitalia to be solely for pleasure, but rather, she was created from his ribs. This is from his chest to know the creator, God, and near his heart to be loved and love God. Eve was created from Adam as the same flesh and blood to make them similar so that sex and marriage between them are pure and proclaim the purity of the Creator God. It is one thing saying with mouth you are an atheist, but to play it out by marrying a stranger is way more convicting. God says, **"Religious confusion is worse than being killed."** (2:191).

The Prophet and his companions, being from marriages of cousins, meant they were pure enough to be suitable for being born and living around the House of God in Mecca. It was also easy for them to accept and spread the pure message of Islam. Ali (raa) was born inside the House of God and from a cousin marriage; his parents were first cousins. Prophet Muhammad (pbuh), also from a cousin marriage, was born in the Year of the Elephant. This was the year when God defended the House of God (Kaaba) from the attack by the African army. God defended His House by using a flock of birds which threw stones at the army, leaving them, as the Quran says, **"like chewed hay."** (105:5).

Prophet Muhammed's (pbuh) father died when his mother was pregnant with him, and his mother died when he was a young child, so they never had sex while he was alive. This is purity and a sign of a pure God, so the Quran says the prophet believed in God, which is mentioned in the Quran to a point.

God is one, so creation must come from parents who are one and similar, such as cousins. This is to avoid contradicting religion. God says respecting the symbols of God is a sign of strong belief. The Quran says blessed is God, the best creator, so creation needs to be pure.

God is the Almusawer, meaning one who forms images, and it is one of God's ninety nine beautiful names. This is manifest in that God creates images and pictures to explain, such as how cousin marriage helps people understand the purity of God.

Divorce is bad because of the importance of cousin marriage, as it is a sign of the existence of God. Not knowing God is the greatest disability a person can suffer from. Being pure and knowledgeable of God by being born from cousin marriage means the person, like the Prophet, is acceptable to God and the angels.

Prophet Muhammed (pbuh) said, "**The best thing in the world is a pious wife**" (Muslim), a relationship of godly meaning. Traditionally, Arab men kill those who marry their cousin, taking her away. It was acceptable self-defence in Arab and Islamic laws.

In Islamic law, there is a concept of "Wald Alfirash" (lit. The child of the bed). This refers to when a married cousin couple faces a situation where the woman performs adultery with a stranger. The child born is given the identity of her cousin's husband so he can benefit from their marriage as a sign of God. They see the benefit of knowing God as more important than the child knowing their birth father. The rules of identity in humans are different from those for expensive horses and cows, not based on sperm but on the relation that proves God.

Three examples of evil in Arabs, where the child is not born from a cousin marriage, so they don't know the good God, include:

1. Abu Lahab was Prophet Muhammed (pbuh)'s paternal uncle. He was born to a father from the Arab tribe of Quraish and a mother from the tribe of Khuzaha. He hated the pure religion of Islam, showed great intolerance and attacked Prophet Muhammed

(pbuh) and his followers. Therefore, God promised him and his wife, hellfire in the Quran.
2. Musilimah the Liar was a false prophet from the tribe of Hanif in Arabia. He first claimed he was a partner to Prophet Muhammed (pbuh) in his prophethood, so Prophet Muhammed (pbuh) called him a liar. His full name is Musilimah, son of Habib (meaning lover); he wasn't born from cousin marriage. In his religion, he banned cousin marriage and allowed fornication. He himself had a famed sexual relationship with an Arab woman from the tribe of Tamim.
3. Osama bin Laden, an evil terrorist who orchestrated the 9/11 attacks in America, where aeroplanes hit the twin towers. Osama's parents were from different tribes and locations. His mother was from the Levant, and his father was from Yemen.

When a child is born and finds there is a better wife for his father, such as a close cousin, it means God doesn't exist for the child. For this reason, men should carefully choose a wife, with a preference for the purest relationship that supports the existence of God.

As cousin marriage is a sign of God, all marriages need to be made famous in Islam, so all people know that God exists. Also, since the virginal couple will be having to touch the harmful genitalia, this means they become dangerous, and people need to be warned about it. Another reason introduced is that children will be born, so the woman is not to be harmed emotionally and physically when pregnant. People should help their children when their parents can't, such as in the case of an illness. In the past, those married to strangers in shame eloped to live on the outskirts of town.

Chapter 4

Heterosexuality

Arabs traditionally considered the marriage of cousins to be a straight heterosexual relationship, while marriage with strangers was considered to be a minor or hidden homosexuality. This is because while they may be male and female in the body, meaning being strangers is a joining of different, so it is impure. The impure human part is the anus, so the stranger woman is like an anus meaning homosexuality. Still, since it is only in meaning and not physical, it's a minor homosexuality or hidden homosexuality.

The cousin marriage is pure since it is a joining of similar people and a joining in the relationship of the father's brother, which contains good meanings of purity and lack of harm. Father from further since anything difficult and further is returned to the father. Brother is from bother because even when they are different gender they share the same parents. Since parents are those who correct problems for the child and the place that needs correction is the genitalia, it is like they are similar in the body even when different genders, so there is a bother. The relation of the cousin, the father and the brother is thus like further of the bother. Therefore, it means lack of harm, and thus, the uncle is called uncle from 'un kill', meaning to give life, and that is why cousins marry, in the relation of the uncle. Hence, they give life in the meaning of un kill.

The word "mother" is perhaps from the word "more do are" because mothers do a lot for the child. In Arabic, the mother is called "youma" from words meaning "touches a lot". This is because the mother, cleans the child, feeds the child, warms the child, hugs the child and entertains the child. In other words, they do a lot to the child or touch them a lot. The sister is probably from the words "is tear are", those who get upset, such as from the brother who bothers her much. This means marriage from aunt's daughter is also pure since the meaning of sadness at the idea of mother, who touches a lot. This state of lack of touch in aunt is therefore purity for the wedding and children. The aunt is probably from "un not", meaning yes and agreeing, because the aunt has no ill intentions due to having ideas of furthering the bother.

When a person is heterosexual and attracted to the opposite gender only, they would want only a cousin marriage. The children of strangers come from different parents, so they know the joining of different, which is a reminder of the joining of the genitalia, which are different in the act of sex. However, since they are reminded by their parents continuously of sex, not only are they in a state of impurity, but they are from different, and so want the same, so they become inclined to homosexuality.

In banning cousin marriage, Muslimah, the liar, is perhaps the first to start heterophobia.

It is the case that cousin marriage gives innocent children, but stranger marriage gives children who know sex from birth. This is because children of strangers, their blood and flesh are different, and their marriage is the coming of different, a clue to the act of sex where the different genitalia are joined. This means children of strangers know sex from birth, making them impure and dirty. However, cousin marriage is the coming together of similar in blood and flesh, so there is no reminder of sex to the children, so they are born pure and innocent.

Moreover, cousin marriage is the marriage of the father's brother to further bother, so there is no expectation that those who further bother will have a relationship in the bothersome genitalia. This means that children of strangers tire from the idea of different joining from their parents and so do not want to marry and have heterosexual sex themselves. However, children of cousin marriages know nothing of differences in body and are not clued into the act of sex, so they become keen and curious about it. This is why people in the past who married cousins often married their children young, as they were deeply curious and hadn't had a clue about sex; it was a human right to know how people were created. This doubt they have about sex can be called erotic scepticism.

This means that strangers marrying is paedophilia since it teaches children the act of sex from a young age and gives paedophiles an excuse to further interact with children sexually. God prohibits such acts as they are inhumane; therefore, the God of Islam commands cousin marriage in the Quran. Those who keep emphasising differences between men and women and oppress women base it on the differences in genitalia; thus, they are rude and shameful. Islam believes in equality between men and women. Prophet Muhammed (pbuh) said, "**Women are the other half of men**" (Tirmizi), meaning they are similar and equal to them.

Homosexuality is forbidden in Islam for four main reasons:

1. Homosexuality begets no children, and so it is anti-life. Prophet Lott, who was sent to guide his people away from homosexuality, has a name that means "what gives" in Arabic, meaning what has benefit, because what gives the child is heterosexuals sex.
2. Homosexuality is a relationship in the anus, so it's impure and dirty, and Islam teaches cleanliness and purity because God is pure.
3. Gay sex humiliates men. When one man assumes the position traditionally held by women, of taking and being given. Islam teaches Muslims, especially men, that they should be dignified. God says in the Quran "**pride is for God, His messenger and the believers.**" (63:8).
4. Homosexuality is against God, since cousin marriage is pure it gives evidence to existence of pure God, but homosexuality is impure relation and so it gives no support to existence of God and so it supports atheism. This is because marriage is a way of creating, and creating in purity supports the existence of a pure creator but creating in impurity does not support a pure creator, so it is atheism. The human face has a nose that looks male and a mouth that looks female, without joining, so the face is a sign of God. Therefore, human design supports heterosexuality and makes homosexuality unnatural and strange and against signs of God.

Homosexuals are killed in Islam because sex is the way of bringing life, and when there is an error, it is a symbol of wanting death, so homosexuality, is an error in sex since it brings no children, is impure and is a symbol of death. A homosexual who admits to their homosexuality is seen as frightening and threatening people with death, and that they may be killed, so God commanded for them to be killed instead by the government. It is like a man carries a knife towards you, and you decide to shoot them before they kill you. However, this punishing game with the meaning of life is not confined to homosexuals; even heterosexuals who commit adultery and thus belittle the importance of correctly giving life are also punished with death in Islam. This is how strictly Islam views playing with life, and many of those who enter cousin marriages do not wish to engage in hidden homosexuality, knowing well how proper homosexuality is perceived by God and how it is punished in the laws of many Muslim and non-Muslim cultures countries.

In Sudan, those married to strangers have a phrase, which is "men are cousins of women", to say as long as they are physically male or female, they are heterosexual, so to accept them socially and religiously as straight.

The child of stranger marriages is also more inclined towards homosexuality, while the child of cousin marriage is strongly heterosexual. This is because the child of stranger marriages has different parents, and they keep enforcing the sex act that joins different genitalia. From this constant emphasis on being different, they become bored and irritated by the differences between men and women and consequently become more excited and interested in relationships based on similarities, which implies homosexuality.

In Islam and among Arabs, homosexuality is not only considered in terms of same-gender relationships but even a relationship between a man and a woman can be labelled as homosexuality. Prophet Muhammad (pbuh) said that even a man who penetrates a woman in her anus is engaging in "minor homosexuality" (Alaini). Marrying strangers is seen as hidden homosexuality because they appear heterosexual, but in meaning and symbolism, they are homosexual. The Quran states, "**God prohibits immoralities, both hidden and apparent**" (7:33)

The Quran also discusses "*uli Albaab*," which is the name of those who appreciate inner and hidden meanings. In one verse, God says, "**In the creating of the heavens and earth, and the differing between the night and day are signs of God for those who appreciate hidden meanings**" (3:190). The word *Albaab* comes from the word *lub*, which means kernel or nuts.

Some think giving a man a choice between girls is a form of praise. Being allowed to check out many girls and choose what attracts him is seen as a pleasure rather than being fated to the cousin regardless of what she is like.

Women who are strangers carry meanings of harm, so they are likened to an anus. Men who are strangers carry meanings of harm, which reduces them from their state of being men. The stranger man has ideas of harm, and men should be perfect and good; thus, it seems as if he is lesser, like a woman or girl, and not a proper man. Cousins, who carry meanings of purity, cleanliness, and grace, are essentially more womanly or manly. If meanings of harm enter a relationship, then they are allowed to divorce, making it difficult to argue that strangers who marry with ideas of harm have a valid marriage.

God prohibits brother-sister relations as it is like homosexuality. This is because they share the same parents who fix their problems, and the place of harm that needs fixing is the genitalia. This means even when different in genders, they share the same parents, so it's like they have the same genitalia. To mean the same genders even when different. God also prohibits marrying father and mother, as they are creators, and impurity to parents says impure creator God likewise sisters and brothers of parents are prohibited.

The Rainbow has a different colour and is bent. To say different is no good, so it means and supports similarities. That's why it is used as a homosexual symbol. The real rainbow in the sky is to remind of cousin marriage who are similar and compatible since their union is a sign of God. The Prophet Muhammed (pbuh) said the rainbow shouldn't be called "the bow of guzah" but instead "the bow of God", adding that guzah is a devil (Abu Naim). This shows how both sides tried to claim the rainbow as a symbol.

Some married to strangers insist their relationship is heterosexual because they are male and female. They give superiority to the body; they have a material literalist view of the world. The main spread of stranger marriage was when Wahhabism/Salafism spread in Arabia. The spread of Salafism/Wahhabism, who have a literal view of God, believing that God has a literal hand and is physically on the throne above the heavens, means they have a body definition of gender.

Muslimah the Liar, whose Salafism came from his region and his descendants, wanted material possessions from Prophet Muhammed (pbuh), the Arabian land. Literalists who take a physical understanding of things marry strangers. Those who obsess over the body by denying marriage to strangers are committing homosexuality and can offend Africans, who have a deep appreciation for life and protect their bodies; thus, they may be harmed by them. This is because they mock Africans and are mischievous. They see them as interfering in African issues yet may provide misinformation that harms people.

Stranger marriage is seen as being an introduction, respect, and starting point to proper homosexuality. God says not to follow in the footsteps of the devil. In the spread of stranger marriage, there is more support for homosexuality and trans culture in our time. Some men marry strangers as they carry meanings of the anus, and it is all the homosexuality the law of some countries permits them. Others see it as a challenge that even if they marry a stranger, they will not gradually desire to marry a man and do homosexuality. Those who enter stranger marriages do so because they are homosexual but find it difficult to practice anal sex. This is especially true in conservative countries, where they marry an unfamiliar woman to get used to that idea, as they are overwhelmed with the fear of homosexuality with men.

Girls who have a lesbian inclination may enjoy the sex between their brothers and other girls. This is like sex by proxy. It is as if they slept with them, they claim. It is like those who have penis envy and wish to have a penis so as to deep penetrate women.

Some use marriage to strangers as a scientific analogy, as a way to explain HIV. In the same way that they accept harm from strangers and don't defend against it, they have no defence against strangers. This is like AIDS, where the virus attacks the immunity, and there is no longer a defence from foreign microbes, so the person becomes ill and dies.

Gay pride is an extreme view of male and male relationships. There is more strength, money, and power, so they feel pride. They are called gay because they are happy. The Quran says, **"God** doesn't like the happy," (28:76) and Prophet Muhammed (pbuh) is described as being sad quite often. Gay pride ideas consider men who have relationships with females to be weaker, poorer, and less dignified. Muslims accept the concept of zuhd as being content with little as a form of expressing heterosexuality. As for lesbians, they refuse men and their giving and so are called lesbians, possibly from the words "less being". God says, "**Don't forget your share of the riches of this world.**" (28:77).

In Islam, men are encouraged to grow their beards. This is because it symbolises purity and cousin marriage. The hair of the beard is devoid of feeling and grows on the lower jaw, meaning the meeting of the two jaws while speaking, eating, or resting is made pure by the hair. This joining of similar jaws is symbolises the joining of cousins who are similar in flesh and blood, since they are part of the same family.

Prophet Lot said to the homosexual men in his time to instead "**marry my daughters, it is more purer**"(11:78). This means a man must always look for the purest relationship. The homosexuals in the time of Prophet Lot said "**throw them, Lot and the straight people out of the village, they are people of purity**" (27:56). This perhaps is the oldest known record of heterophobia in the world.

Chapter 5

Innocent Children

Children are usually born innocent. They are born without puberty, without sexual desire, and sexual characteristics such as breasts, armpits or pubic hair. This can be understood as a natural command for them to be kept innocent and without sexual suggestion or sexual acts. Innocence is a beauty, like honour and chastity, and so it gives beauty to the child, making their parents want to see, touch, and care for them. Innocence is purity and cleanliness; thus, children are superior in their closeness to angels and God; traditionally, people used to ask children to pray for them. The child's innocence is also the basis for their honour and chastity when they grow up and marry.

The child of a cousin marriage is born innocent, but the child of strangers is born knowing about sex. This is because children of cousin marriages are born from parents who are similar in flesh and blood, so their coming together in marriage is a joining of similarity and, consequently, purity. The parents, similar in flesh and blood, allude to similarities in body and so do not expose the idea that they are different in body, in the case of the genitalia. This means the child of a cousin marriage is not aware of the differences. The genitalia from their parents and neither the sexual act, which is the joining of the different genitalia.

However, the children of strangers and their parents are different in flesh and blood, which is a joining of differences, and this reminds us of the joining of the genitalia, which is different and opposite. This means the child of strangers is clued to sex, that there are differences in men and women, and that the genitalia are made to join just as their parents who are different have been joined in marriage. This is impurity, making them impure. This is dangerous since it encourages paedophilia and sexual acts against children, as they believe the child already knows about sex from their parents who are different and joined, so their paedophilia is then considered nothing major. It is also incest, as it is the parents who tell the child about sex repetitively through their act of joining in a marriage when they are strangers and different. This means that when the child grows older, they might even be sexually aroused by their parents.

The cousin marriage has the benefit of being from the uncle, the father's brother. The description of the father's brother, meaning further of the bother, is important in the innocence of the children. When parents are cousins, and thus they are in a relationship of the further of bother, then no one, especially the child, knows that they practise a relationship of sex in the bothersome area of the genitalia. This denial of sex acts as a protection of the child from the paedophilia of the parents. In stranger marriage, the children know so much about sex from their parents that some parents become sexually attracted to their children and have physical sex with them. In early Islam, a man who had sex with his mother was killed by Prophet Mohammed (pbuh). Arabs before Islam used this denial of sexual acts as a protection for the child from the paedophilia of the parents. Prior to Islam, Arabs used to murder their daughters out of fear of scandal stemming from stranger marriages. Aisha means "will live", as she was born from cousin marriage. The killed girl was called "Mawuda", meaning "I don't love her", as their father buried them in shame so that no one would consider if they had sexual relations with them. The Quran mentions this phenomenon, stating, **"When people ask why the Mawuda was killed,"** (81:8-9), the reason being that they were from a stranger marriage.

The act of sex usually stems from the sexual desire that is initiated by the presence of a person of the opposite sex. However, sexual desire begins after puberty when secondary sexual characteristics start to appear, such as the enlargement of the genitalia and the development of breasts. This means that, naturally, the act of sex is for adults and not for children. The genitalia are not only a place of excrement but also a frightening aspect to consider, even for adults. The act of sex, which involves the joining of different and opposite genitalia, is an act of impurity that requires a ritual bath in Islam afterwards. It is thus inhumane, insensitive, and should be illegal to introduce children to sex in the marriage of strangers. Some trivialise this by asserting that it is only thoughts and not physical sex; however, in Islam, one of God's names is "Al Lateef," meaning The Gentle, so even hints or meanings matter to God.

The Quran says that Muslims should be gentle and soft. In one verse, **"His heart has sinned"** (2:283), and in another, **"some thoughts are sinful"** (49:12), and **"Saved are those who come to God with a**

sound heart" (26:89). This means to have a mind filled with good ideas and thoughts, rather than with sex and atheism. That thinking needs to be correct. The chapter of the Cow says God will account for thoughts, physical actions, and deeds. When the child is born from cousin marriage, they cease to know about sex, since parents are similar, and so they remain innocent until they themselves marry and have sex and then find out there are differences between genders and discover the act of sex after being doubtful of its existence. However, the child born from strangers has been told that people different in bodies join into a marriage union or are clued into sex where various parts of bodies are joined. This means they are born knowing about sex, and every time they consider their parents, they also consider the idea of sex.

If the child considers their parents every fifteen minutes and is therefore clued into the act of sex, then this can amount to around a hundred sexual thoughts in a day, three thousand a month, thirty-five thousand a year, and three million in a lifetime. All these thoughts about sex leave the person not only with sexual desire and a dirty mind but also with impurity, which makes their worship of the pure God of Islam problematic. Impurity that is unstable in the person, such as farting or a period, is a temporary impurity lifted by washing. Still, the impurity of being from two tribes or races and ideas of sex is permanent. God says in the Quran, "**After performing the rituals of Hajj, mention God by repeating his name as much as one mentions their fathers, or even with greater intensity**" (2:200). This shows that God acknowledges that people remember their parents much in the world. The child, from the first day they are born, has 100 thoughts of sex; that is like a young man on his honeymoon. Normally, millions of thoughts are only achieved in eternal heaven. This means the child is like an adult from childhood. Thought about his parents every 15 minutes is just a random number; babies and children think more about their parents, as they depend on them for many things, like food, cleaning, protection, and entertainment.

The child of a cousin marriage has similar parents, so there is no telling of the differences between the man and woman in the genitalia. This means the child at puberty gains a state of doubt about the existence of the opposite gender. This is why, in Arabic, puberty is called "Morahaga", literally 'Are women real?'. This is because traditionally, Arabs married cousins, and their children did not perceive the existence of the genders. Since everyone covered up, they doubted if women and their genitalia were real. This state is then fulfilled when they get married and are exposed to female genitalia for the first time. This doubt is a pleasure since it is a form of extreme chastity and honour. Girls also doubt the existence of men when born from cousin marriage, so they are of great purity, and this is a pleasure to them and their husbands. This doubt is further strengthened by the fact that people cover their genitalia with clothes, so no one knows for sure the real difference between the genitalia of women and men until after marriage. However, children of strangers can have no curiosity, as their parents spoil sex for them from the time they are children.

In Muslim countries where women cover head to toe, this means there is greater doubt in the boys as to the existence of females. However, this shouldn't be so extreme that women and men become a strange reality, worthy of destruction or harm, and this doesn't happen as a person lives at home with both parents and siblings of different genders, so no one becomes too extreme in their doubt of the opposite gender.

In communities where people commonly marry strangers, where people don't cover well, and where there is easy access to pornography, all leads to a lack of this gender doubt. So they don't find much pleasure in the discovery of the opposite gender on their wedding night, simply as they already have knowledge of the differences between genders and their existence in society. The emphasis on the different genders and the act of sex from parents over a long time leaves the child from stranger marriage desensitised, making them insensitive to sexual stimuli, meaning a man can see a naked woman or hear sexual material and not become aroused nor get sexual desire, and this leads to a decreased pleasure in sex.

In English, the word "marry" can mean to be wed but is also used to express surprise. This shows that historically, early Europeans who married cousins were aware the idea of sex socked them.

A child from a cousin marriage is perpetually innocent and doesn't know the difference between genders for sure since they were created from a pure relation of similarities. This means a man from a cousin marriage, even after he has sex with his wife and becomes exposed to her genitalia and touches it, his nature overwhelms and afterwards is again in doubt if women truly exist since parents are cousins and created not knowing parents are different and so doesn't know for sure genders exist.

This state of return to virginity even after having sex, Prophet Muhammed (pbuh) said in heaven the women return physically back to virginity after every sexual act, meaning the hymen regrows again after sex and God is capable of all things. However, a man born from strangers is born knowing there are differences between men and women since parents are strangers, and so are different in body (in flesh and blood), and so is not a virgin even before the act of sex. After the act of sex, they do not again gain a state of innocence and purity.

Arabs call relationships between strangers *Aar*, meaning nakedness; since the parents are different, they emphasise the place of difference, meaning the genitalia, so it is as if they are naked or practising sex without a cover. In English, it is called elope, possibly from ill-low-be, since it is emphasis on the lower part of the body.

It is the case that people can intentionally create children not from cousin marriage, for instance, to lower losses during times of war. This is because the child of strangers is born knowing sex and so is a victim of paedophilia. Children are born atheists; they don't know God and are thus seen as inferior, and their loss won't be great. It is a tactic of war; they don't give an advantage to the enemy by allowing them to kill good people from cousin marriage. This is the case in Europe, where the two world wars turned societies that even detest cousin marriage to encourage strangers to marry and produce children whose loss in war will be easy to accept and to produce those who will find it easy in their hearts to kill others in war. They also married strangers to show they were strong and tough in war, to demonstrate they had no mercy. In the West, children of cousin marriages are modernly insulted to be inbred and children of incest. When inbred and incest are when there is random mating between relatives of the first degree, but cousin marriage is programmed and specific to cousin only. This is because, in Islam, there is an explicit prohibition in the Quran against the marriage of the sister, mother, aunt, grandmother, and niece. God says in the Quran, **"Men are forbidden to marry their mothers, their daughters, and their sisters. Also, their father's sister, and their mother's sister, and daughter of their brother and daughter of their sister. Also** forbidden, the mothers of their wives, and daughters of their wives, if their marriage is not consummated, then it is lawful to marry their daughters. Likewise forbidden, wives of their son from their own bodies, and to marry sisters except if one marriage was cancelled, and God is forgiving and merciful" (4:23).

The fact that a child of strangers is provoked by harmful experiences from knowing sex from parents and not knowing God; therefore, their punishment is seen as unjust. This means the abolishment of capital punishment and other severe punishments around the world where they don't marry cousins. This is simply because they can't deal with it, being on top of their suffering from being from stranger marriage, and also since it is their nature which is provoking them to commit these crimes, it is seen it is unfit to punish them.

Traditionally, in Arab and Muslim cultures, they believed that a cousin child is more dignified, respected, and considered prouder than children from stranger marriages. It is very common in Sudan to say, "So and so is invincible because their parents are paternal cousins", or for a person to praise themselves by saying they are born from cousins. In Sudanese Arabic, they call children "jahil" (lit. Ignorant), meaning one who doesn't know about sex and marriage.

Gender role stereotypes suggest that women cook, clean, and stay at home raising the children, while men leave the house to work and provide for the family. This was traditionally seen as a cover for admitting to sexual desire as a main reason to marry. Children who see parents adhering to gender roles also become shielded from sexual ideas expressed by parents. There are important reasons for their parents to be together; they rely on each other. A woman wants a man to protect and provide for her, while a man wants a woman who can cook, do his laundry, and safeguard his belongings at home.

In Arabic, the mother is "youma," meaning one who touches a lot. This is because the mother touches the baby, cleaning, feeding, and playing with them. Maternal uncle in Arabic is called "khal," from words meaning "disgusting no," since he is a brother or bother to the mother, meaning touch without harm. This means children from maternal cousins are also protected from sexual ideas from their parents. The greater the similarities between parents, the greater the child is protected against sexual ideas. Ali (raa)'s parents were first cousins, and even the meanings of their fathers are similar. His mother was Fatimah, daughter of Asad, and his father, Abu Taleb, son of Abdu Almutalib; Asad means lion, and Mutalib means need. Since lions are symbols of need and greed, this means both his grandparents had similar name meanings. This is why Ali (raa) was the first child to become a Muslim believer in Mecca. God says in the Quran, "**In heaven, men will have partners that were not oversexed by humans or jinn.**" (55:56). This means they see sex as something new, strange or interesting. To be oversexed by Jinn means they had too many sexual thoughts and emotions.

God says in the Quran, "**He did not make people witness their own creation.**" (18:51). This is because spirit is gained a few months after conception in the womb. This is also a command to marry cousins and not to marry strangers who expose the sex act to their children and society.

Tahneek uses chewed dates to rub the baby's palate after birth. Prophet Muhammed (pbuh) did this. It is a prophecy to the child that there are sweet things in life and that the child should be introduced to sweet and good things.

Hassan and Hussain, the grandsons of Prophet Muhammad (peace be upon him), one of them urinated on the lap of Prophet Muhammed (pbuh), so his uncle's wife, Um Alfadul, hit the baby. Prophet Muhammad (peace be upon him) said to her, **"Don't hurt my child."** (Ibn Maja). There are principles of mercy to children in Islam. The Prophet Muhammed (pbuh) said, **"he is not one of us Muslims who doesn't show children mercy or elderly respect."** (Alnawawi). Prophet Muhammed (pbuh) said, **"Show mercy to those on earth; those in heaven will show you mercy."** (Alsuti).

Arabs name their sons Saeed, meaning "lucky", and daughters Saeeda, also meaning "lucky", because they believe they are fortunate to be born of cousins and thus know God, remaining pure and innocent from molestation.

Prophet Muhammad (pbuh) commanded that as soon as a child can differentiate between their right and left hand, they should not sleep with their parents, as they start to understand the two genders and will understand them if they have sex. Children have a right to innocence and should have no knowledge or act regarding sex, whether explicit or implicit. God says, **"Do not kill your children"** (17:31), so parents should refrain from stranger marriages in order not to cause harm to their children.

Other than cousin marriage, God allows a man to marry an enslaved person he owns or a damsel in distress called (heba). Heba is marriage to a woman whose circumstances require marriage to strangers. This could be because she is an orphan, fleeing war, an immigrant, or does not have cousins; she is married to a stranger to find help and protection in life. Cousin marriage is about doing good, and so when a relationship between strangers is aimed at doing good, it is acceptable in Islam. Just as in the absence of water, people use the earth to purify, the ill do not fast, or one may eat pig, when without other food. Likewise, Islam recognises when strangers marry for mutual benefit, forced by circumstances to accept strangers in marriage. Kids from these marriages know there is an improvement in their parents from marriage, so they don't consider they will have a relationship with dirty genitalia. To show mercy is allowed in Islam. The Prophet Muhammed (pbuh) was sent to be a mercy to the world, warning and saving them from the eternal hellfire. Likewise, a child from an enslaved person recognises his father as owning his mother. Since owners protect their belongings and don't let harm befall them, again, the child doesn't accept parents' touch in place of harm, meaning having sex by joining genitalia.

The Quran says Mary (as), the mother of Jesus, was sceptical when the angel came to give her a son while she was a virgin. She said, **"How can I have a child while no man has touched me?"** (19:20). In a natural state, Arab/Muslim children born from cousins exhibit this sexual scepticism. The idea of different male and female genitalia and their union in sex are new concepts to them, as parents are similar in blood and flesh and do not realise the differences between people. Arabs believe the best gain in life isn't gold, diamonds, and rubies, but rather human life, the new baby. Humanity is special and dignified in the sight of God and is better than all of God's other creations. This is why murder is regarded as a great sin, and the Quran states that it is like killing all of humanity because all of humanity is hurt in sympathy even when one person is killed and dies. Children are born scared of strangers, and adults have no interest in sex or marriage with strangers.

Sex is a mighty thought; it is disgusting, frightening, tiresome and impure. This is all too much on children. Only God is a bigger idea in the head than sex. God says, pray, "**Lord, don't burden us with that we are incapable of bearing**" (2:286).

Because sex is important for life, it can't be denied when established, like with children born from strangers.

Quran says Jesus (as) spoke as a baby defending his mother's honour, which shows that children from a young age understand these ideas and are affected by them, even if they can't speak and express themselves like Jesus (as) did.

God says in the Quran, "**We did not make them witness how they were created**", meaning a person shouldn't be told about how they were created, meaning by sex, and so this verse prohibits marriage of strangers where a child gets to know about sex.

God is gentle as one of His beautiful names, so even gentle thoughts and ideas are accountable to God.

In one Hadith, Prophet Muhammed (pbuh) said hundreds of thousands of angels curse the person who ponders on other people's genitalia. In stranger marriages, children are forced to consider their parent's genitalia and their act of sex based on the description that they are different and joined as a couple.

The child should not know the sex between parents, as parents are the creators of the child; they become a symbol of the Creator, who is God. For this reason, Islam honours parents and teaches respect and obedience towards parents. Prophet Muhammed (pbuh) said, "**Heaven lies under the feet of the mother.**" (Alzurgani).

The Prophet Muhammed (pbuh) commanded a prohibition on "Images." This is often misunderstood as camera pictures, but even water casts a picture. The Prophet Muhammed (pbuh) is said to have looked in a water vase to see himself. The real prohibition on images is that the marriage of strangers helps people imagine, consider, and accept atheism, sex, and paedophilia.

Kindness, intelligence, and thoughtfulness are sexy and beautiful, especially for Arabs living in the harsh desert. This meant that traditionally, cousins are strongly attracted to each other, knowing their relationship is beneficial to children, fosters positive ideas, and supports God and Islam. Famous love stories in Arabs are between cousins such as Anter and Abla, Gais and Laila, and Prophet Muhammed (pbuh) and Lady Aisha.

The Quran considers sexualised children; God says, "**children who have not been exposed to the genitalia of women.**" (24:31). These children the Quran states that women do not need to cover in front of them. So the Quran differentiates between children who know about sex and those who don't, and women need to cover from the latter to avoid further sexualising them. This abundance of sexual ideas for children is so overwhelming that it feels almost physical. Mental abuse is as significant as physical abuse.

The animal that most represents harm is the dog; it finds fault in everything, is in much harm and barks a lot. For this reason, it is impure. In a culture of strangers, children with the most harm and abuse, people show love for dogs to say they accept people of much harm. Prophet Muhammed (pbuh) said a prostitute would enter paradise because she gave water to a thirsty stray dog.

Women are known to be gentle, polite, kind and merciful, so they cannot accept hurting children, especially their own. Prophet Muhammed (pbuh) said women of his tribe of Qurish are the kindest Arab women to their children. This is possible because they are stricter about marrying cousins, like his own mother, who married her cousin even before God revealed it in the Quran.

Black hair and white skin are the look of the people of Heaven, but Arabs prefer brown skin since there is no contrast of opposites, so a person doesn't know if opposites can meet. For this reason, Sudanese Arabs, who have brown skin, are proud and consider themselves very Arab and pure, as they have no contrast of colours between hair and skin. Interestingly, most of them descend from Prophet Muhammed's (pbuh) family.

People of Paradise have a contrasting look, as Heaven is a place of gain, and the gain of children comes from the meeting of opposites. Prophet Muhammed (pbuh) said, "**Beware of the green-blooded women**" (Ibn Almulgin), and when asked who they were, he said the girl who was beautiful but had a bad upbringing. Such a girl knows of sex, and her look of black hair and white skin also expresses the meeting of opposites, meaning sex. Prophet Muhammed (pbuh) is loved by God, for he was born in purity and lived a pure life. Prophet Muhammed (pbuh) prayed, "**Lord, just like You made my body beautiful, make my character beautiful**" (Ahmed).

In Islam, when Prophet Muhammed (pbuh) is mentioned, we pray and say, peace be upon him, because the Quran says, "**God and His angels send blessings upon Muhammed. Those who believe should likewise send him peace and blessings**" (33:56). This is because Muhammed was a pure man. He was born to parents who were cousins; he married cousins and married his children to cousins. In Sudan, they curse "may God not know you," meaning not pure, so God ignores them, leading to unanswered prayers, no blessings, and damnation.

Children are to be kept safe since sex finds pleasure in harm. It's a dangerous concept for kids who need to avoid all harm to stay safe. When a child becomes post-puberty, they are no longer considered children but adults. This modern way of categorising adulthood as late teens means there are puberty children with sexual desires and, menstruation and the ability to get pregnant, all placed in the same category as truly innocent young children, which is a danger for them. Children are weak and need to be careful; God says in the Quran, "**The human was created weak.**" (4:28). When a child of a stranger cries, it is not known what their reason is; some fear it could be because they understood the sexual abuse.

If sex is not physical, just ideas, it is still powerful, for it is a sensitive issue. Prophet Muhammed (pbuh) said, "**The eye fornicates and the genitalia either believes it's true sex or considers it a lie**" (Ibn Hazm), meaning desire is aroused from sight. Intense sexual desire and suggestions arouse and can become physical, such as erection or lubricant release in women. If a man talks about football, his foot doesn't normally kick; if a girl talks about food, her hand doesn't normally raise to her mouth, but sexual thought causes physical changes in humans. This means that sexual ideas should not be ignored and be directed towards children, so cousin marriage is the best choice for them. Prophet Muhammad (pbuh) said, "**Choose well for your children, so marry compatible women and marry your daughters to compatible men.**" (Ibn Maja). In modern times, it is misunderstood as marrying for physical attributes such as pretty eyes, light skin, or long hair, when it actually means choosing cousin marriage to safeguard children against sexual ideas, as well as mental and physical sexual abuse.

The Quran states that children need to knock and seek permission before entering their parents' room at certain times of the day so as not to witness sexual activity accidentally.

Crucifixion is the act of nailing people to a wooden cross; wood symbolises the need for water, as trees need it, and the cross represents the joining of opposites, such as sex, so the total meaning is purity or the lack of sexual activity. Killing on the cross is intended to teach purity to the extent of death. The Quran states that Jesus was not killed on the cross, as he was pure, born from a virgin without sexual relations.

Pornography is derived from the word "born," meaning to show people how they are created. This type of pornography is popular among Christians, as they believe in Jesus being born from a virgin, which confuses some into using pornography out of curiosity, while others do so to arouse themselves and masturbate. In Sudan, it is rumoured that Arabs used to allow people to watch the sexual activity between the bride and groom for those curious about their creation through cousin marriage or wanting to understand how people are conceived. It is very sad and unjust that Prophet Muhammed (pbuh), who came from a cousin marriage, married cousins and married his children to cousins, and came with the Quran that commands cousin marriage to save children from sexual abuse, is modernly attacked for marrying his cousin Aisha at a young age. Prophet Muhammed (pbuh) is the only Prophet and man in history to defend children from paedophilia, so to accuse him of it is very disgusting and unfair.

Chapter 6

The Sane Mind

Arabs are a human race that lives in the desert of the Arabian Peninsula. The harsh, dangerous desert means that the Arabs see themselves as a race that identifies as representing the mind and the fact that humans have mental understanding. This is because a person needs to be careful, thoughtful, and mindful to survive in the desert. The Quran says, "**God sent the Quran in Arabic so people could easily understand the message**" (12:2). This is because Arabic is a language that expresses ideas to preserve a good mental state. Omar (raa) is quoted as having said, "**Learning the Arabic language increases intelligence.**"

The Arabs considered cousin marriage to stem from sane minds and that cousin marriage supports sanity. This is because cousin marriage comes from uncles and aunts, and so it's father's brother, or further of bother, and this supports a healthy mind that prevents harm to the self and others. Arabs traditionally defined mental health as wanting good and avoiding harm, and mental illness as the opposite, meaning wanting harm to the self or others and refusing good things. Cousin marriages strengthen the mind and empowers ideas of safety, survival, and respect for life. Marrying strangers can lead to harmful behaviour that is humiliating and risky. Arabs' desire to survive the desert means they find cousin marriage a must in their culture.

Marriage is seen as a mental test. Those who marry cousins are seen as sane, while those who marry strangers are weak in the mind. The Arabs see the man who marries his cousin as showing mental prowess, whereas a man who marries strangers is seen as stupid or mentally ill. Those who marry cousins are viewed as friendly and kind, while those who marry strangers are considered harmful and dangerous. The marriage of strangers poses great harm to individuals and society, so it doesn't make sense to support it or, worse, to practice it in the world.

God is the greatest idea the mind can ponder, and a child of strangers who doesn't know God in their nature is thus not in an ideal mindset. There are rumours in the Middle East that children of strangers are smarter since, from a young age, their minds think of sex, making them mature like adults, even when they are still children. However, this is not true. The constant exposure to sex for a child from strangers' marriage can also leave the person sad, irritated, and humiliated. These emotions imbalance the mind, so a person finds it difficult to think properly.

Because Arabs are people of the mind, and sanity is about gain and success, they admire men who have flesh in their genitalia and see women as inferior for having emptiness in their genitalia. This is why men can be very handsome, such as the prophet Joseph mentioned in the Quran.

The Sane Mind

Thinking is about realising similarities. When parents are similar, it's a clue about how to think. For example, fruits grow from flowers, and then seeing a fruit basket brings to mind the idea of a bouquet of flowers. The mind is important. If a man becomes mad and attacks another man in self-defence, he could be killed.

People want good minds that are not influenced by stranger marriages. The mind is sensitive, and mental confusion is seen by Arabs as abuse.

In Sudanese Arab tradition, wrong relationships, such as fornication and adultery, are seen as mental illness. It is ruthlessness not to treat them as is done nowadays. Instead of being cured, they are currently considered sophisticated and civilised. Men who wish to express their emotions and desire a love story are not common among men, who are usually serious. Overwhelming love emotions and excessive attachment to strangers could be attributed to jinn (spirits) and a sign of possession. They require exorcism by a scholar reading the Quran over them and drinking Islamic holy water called Zamzam.

Love stories in movies and fairy tales do not depict married life and children. Those who perceive strangers' marriages as romantic stories or fairy tales are very mistaken and must not be sure.

When the Quran or Arabs say men are better than women, it is neither praise nor humiliation. This is because men have flesh in their genitalia, the penis, while women experience absence, the vagina. This suggests men symbolise gain and being given, while women represent absence and destruction. This creates a metaphor and imparts wisdom. Men marry women, and women marry men, so they balance each other in the end. Prophet Muhammad said women are the other half of men.

Marrying cousins affects the mind to help cure madness. It is also believed to restore mischief in young men; they would say, "Just marry him, his paternal cousin." Gais and Layla were Arab cousins, and he became mad with mental illness when his uncle refused to allow him to marry his cousin. His poetry, which expresses his love for his cousin, is renowned among Arabs and Muslims worldwide. For this reason, those not married to cousins are seen as having mental weakness and needing to be watched for their safety. Since sex is the smartest idea for survival, some modernly believe and claim children from strangers knowing sex will make them smarter. They are usually not smart enough to understand themselves, so they do not rebel, hate, or seek revenge on their parents. Their thinking is a problem as there is the danger that they would commit suicide in shame or choose to be killed in disappointment from not knowing God like Ishmael. The truth is that thinking requires a clear mind, and constant reminders of sex can cloud the mind. Therefore, traditionally, Arabs believed children from cousin marriages are the most intelligent.

CHAPTER 7

Honour

Honour is the pride associated with being chaste, faithful, and pure. Chastity is refusing sex when not married, faithfulness is not having sex outside of marriage, and purity is being born from a legitimate marriage. Honour is a beautiful thing indeed; it is a praiseworthy state. Some people even kill to defend their honour.

Cousin marriages are honourable because a woman who marries a cousin restricts sex and marriage to relatives only. However, a woman who is ready to marry any stranger is open to a sexual relationship with any man; this state of promiscuity is like prostitution and thus lacks honour.

Honour is sex being exclusive to a certain man or woman. This preserves bloodlines and gives children a true belonging. This is because if women promote marriage and sex to all men, then a child doesn't know who their father is or their family or racial belonging.

It is strange for a man to have a daughter from his flesh who has sex with all men or a woman to have a daughter who inherits her vagina and for a man, not a cousin, to have sex with it. In honour, men consider their daughters to be from their blood and flesh and touching their daughter's body is like touching the father's and other male relatives' bodies. They thus prefer men they trust and related to them to marry their daughters.

Sometimes, prostitution is hidden by marriage between strangers when prostitution is illegal in a country. Arabs used to think stranger marriages were fornication. As in Arabic, fornication is about touch outside of the plan of genealogy, or in other words, outside the family tree.

Chapter 8

Just Marriage

A just marriage is a marriage that causes no harm to oneself or others. The cousin marriage commanded in the Quran is a just marriage. It does not harm the child or society. However, marriage between strangers is unjust; it is a sin and a crime. This is because marriage between strangers is sexually explicit, as they come together when different, which describes the act of sex where differing genitalia are joined. This teaches the child from a young age about sex and exposes the act of sex to society, offending elders, religious figures, and chaste virgins. For this reason, marriage between strangers is not only harmful to their own children but to society as a whole. Prophet Muhammed warned against discussing what occurs in the bedroom.

When marriage is unlimited and can be with any random woman, a man cannot be trusted with his mother, sister, daughter, aunt, or grandmother. Cousin marriage limits sexual relationships and marriage to cousins only.

A just marriage in the Quran is called Muhsan, while an unjust marriage (meaning between strangers) is referred to as Sifaah. Muhsan comes from a word meaning protected, whereas Sifaah derives from "si fah" (literally harm spread). The Quran commands for Muhsan marriage (just marriage); God says, "**Women should be in Muhsan marriage (just marriage) and not in Sifaah (elopement).**" (4:25) In Sudanese Arabic, Muhsan is called Sutra, meaning covered, and Sifaah is called Aar, meaning naked. Cousin marriage is considered Muhsan because it does not entail harmful ideas, thus protecting those involved. Marriage between strangers is called Sifaah because, by being different, they propagate ideas of genitalia and sex. By making their marriage known, they spread sexual ideas and broadcast them throughout society. God in the Quran states, "**Those who wish to spread sexual immoralities among people who believe in God, for them is a severe punishment in this world and the hellfire**" (24:19). Ali's marriage to Fatima was just. In fact, Ali had to sell his armour, which he used to shield his blessed body in war, to pay for his wedding to Lady Fatimah, his cousin's daughter.

Just like in Islam, yellow clothes are forbidden as yellow symbolises harm, and relationships, where there is a remembering of genitalia and harm, should, as a priority, be forbidden.

Prophet Muhammed (pbuh) prohibited sleeping on the left side. This is to say sex and marriage shouldn't be bad meanings, for the left carries ideas of harm and disgust since it's the left hand used in cleaning the genitalia.

Prophet Muhammed (pbuh) said there will be women who are naked whilst wearing clothes who will not enter heaven. This is because, in a stranger's marriage, the couple is dressed but symbolises different genitalia and sex. Showing genitalia is shameful and humiliating; the Quran speaks about Adam and Eve becoming naked after eating from the prohibited tree. Then, they quickly covered their genitalia with leaves they cut from nearby trees.

When a man has sex with a stranger outside marriage, it is called *zina*, but when a man has sex with a stranger after a marriage ceremony, it is called *sifah* or *arr*.

Since joining the different reminds us of joining the different genitalia in sex, Prophet Muhammed (pbuh) prohibited sitting half under the sun and half under the shade so as not to join the different and be impure. This included he said dates, meaning not to put dates and their stones together or even wearing only one shoe at a time and walking. Prophet Muhammed (pbuh) commanded that men should colour their greys with henna making it yellow, orange, or red, so that there is no contrast and joining of white hair to black hair—a symbol of impurity.

Some people want others to know when they had loved and had sex and prove it by public display of affection. Public nudity is illegal in the world, but mental symbolism is yet to be made illegal.

The consequences of stranger marriages are by knowing them, there is harm; if a child, they take some of his innocence; if a virgin, she loses some of her virginity; if a scholar, it reduces their belief in God; if an older man, they may arouse sexual desire. When they are without physical strength to act on it, a stranger marriage is considered vulgar, explicit and impolite.

In Arab and Muslim cultures, people usually engage in sexual activities in private. This occurs in a home behind a wall, in a room with the door locked, at night, with the light switched off, covered with a blanket, and alone, with curtains drawn close. However, those who marry strangers often find no excitement and, instead, experience boredom from family expectations and long for something new. Some are simply voyeurs and can be described as having agoraphilia, which is the fetish of being public with sex.

CHAPTER 9

Preservation of Bloodline

Death is a terrible thing that we all have to face and endure. However, what if I tell you that you can live again? I don't mean in the afterlife of heaven and earth but in this world. In cousin marriage, there is preservation of the bloodline, meaning there will be the passing of a person's blood from one generation to the next. Thus, another person is created with the original person's eyes, feet, or nose. This means they do not die entirely but live again. However, when strangers marry, the blood is diluted; it is watered down and becomes extinct, so no other person is born again from the bloodline of that original person.

Cousin marriages preserve the characteristics of the father, grandfather and forefathers, but strangers introduce a new look and characteristics to the bloodline. This is corruption, and more so, it is murder to the bloodline. When the new blood is from a different race, it constitutes genocide since no full person from the tribe or race is born again. The Quran says, "**They spoil and corrupt in genealogy and harvest, and God does not like corruption.**" (2:205). Royalty and Prophet Muhammed (pbuh) descendants usually marry cousins and within the family to preserve their good genes and continue their bloodlines. Prophet Mohammed (pbuh) said women would give birth to their brothers and uncles, spoiling the idea that in a stranger marriage, the child can be said to be the father alone.

The Prophet Mohammed (peace be upon him) said, "Make good choices for your children." This is not understood as choosing nice hair or eyes or skin colour, but it means bringing them into the world through a cousin's marriage and ensuring their purity, chastity, goodness, and religion.

The point of birthing a child is to have something of yourself alive, part of you living, so you can say you haven't died out of the world completely. This means a person desires to have a child who is most like them. This is possible with cousin marriage since strangers spoil the bloodline. However, this means no longer similar people are born again into the world.

Chapter 10

The Spirit

The Spirit is not just the soul that leaves the body after death; it is an important part of human life. The spirit is what differentiates us from the animals and other creations of God. The spirit is an understanding of other than the self, of being able to consider others and empathise with other creatures. For instance, if a goat falls into a well, no other goats come to its rescue, regardless of how much sound it makes. However, if a human falls into a well, people gather around him, crying with him in empathy, while others bring ropes to rescue him. This state of humans helping is spirit; it is acknowledging other than the self and showing empathy. The spirit is, thus, essential to human interactions and is the foundation of our kind society.

It is the case that the child of cousin marriage has a strong spirit. This is because spirit is knowledge using relativity. A person measures things relative to themselves; they consider what if it happens to them;

they will be sad, so they empathise when it happens to others. When the child is from a cousin marriage, a child has a sense of oneness since both parents are similar, and they can measure things relative to themselves. However, children of strangers have different parents, so they don't have a pivot of themselves to measure things against. For instance, if a person eats chilli and is hurt, a child of strangers cannot empathise since they can't find oneness with them, as their parents are different and may have various views about chilli.

This lack of empathy and understanding of others by a child of strangers is dangerous, as they become disinhibited and can harm others since they won't empathise with their victim. They simply lack spirit or possess a weak spirit. However, the child of cousin marriage won't harm others as they can empathise with others and their hurt. The lack of cousin marriages in the West means there is a large amount of crime and violence, which is absent in the Middle East, where they practise cousin marriage. It is only recently in the Middle East that they started stranger marriages, causing crime and wars to become normal.

The spirit is unlike the body, which is hard and chunky. The spirit is gentle and light; it is also pure, so it can only exist in the pure relationship of cousin marriage. The emphasis on the act of sex and the genitalia in stranger marriages is not only dirty and impure, but it also removes spirit.

The idea of the goodness of cousin marriage versus that of strangers is a gentle thing of the spirit. In stranger marriage, the parents don't literally suggest genitalia and sexual acts with children do not equate to actual sex; rather, they communicate repetitively through gentle suggestions, being physically different in flesh and blood and united. They embody the roles of genitalia, which differ and connect during sexual activity.

As people who appreciate the spirit and believe in gentleness, especially as life can be hard and harsh at times, we should thus strongly oppose marriages between strangers and support cousin marriage. God says in the Quran, "**The human is created weak**" (4:28). This is true; we are soft in flesh and blood, but we are also gentle in spirit. We are easily offended, and we shouldn't be made to feel sad, inferior, or irritated. We must consider how a child of strangers will feel and hope they do not experience offence. We should also remember that God does not desire their existence due to suffering, which is a form of euthanasia even before they are born. However, in our time, people often oppose the existence of children from cousin marriages due to the claimed risk of genetic disease.

Chapter II

Identity

In a marriage of strangers, there is an identity crisis, and this is because the child is born not knowing God. This means it is difficult to associate them with God, and since they cannot be easily considered to be a creation of God, how can they be said to belong to their parents?

Identity is related to purity. When an apple is covered in mud, you don't know if it's a tennis ball, a rock, or an apple, but if it's clean and pure, you can identify it as an apple. Likewise, a child born from purity has a strong identity, but when born from fornication and impurity, they lose identity.

All of humanity is good and deserves no genocide. As children of Adam, we are all one big family and should be happy. Different races and tribes are a beauty and not a shortcoming that should be erased through mixed-race marriage and children. The existence of different races supports the idea that God loves humans and makes humanity special. For instance, if a new mother is asked about her newborn child, she says, "These are his clothes, this is his hat, this is his bottle, these are his shoes." She counts the different things and is keen to show off her child. Likewise, I believe the different races exhibit different human activities: Africans are people of life, as they defend themselves from a lion or engage in something important for life. Caucasians are people of creation; if they want to accomplish an important task, they will pursue it. Persians are people of prophecy; if they have placed something somewhere before, they may want to retrieve it again. Arabs are people of the mind; if they are thinking about something and making a choice or decision, they are alert to stay safe in the desert. Indians are people of comfort as they rest, while Chinese are people of restoration, striving to repair something or help someone.

Now, a man in the desert, when he wakes up and has food, it is like African nature. Then, when he decides to take his clothes from the cupboard, it is like Persian nature. When he decides to choose which camel to sell, that reflects Arab nature. When he decides to fetch water from a well, it is Caucasian in nature. When he attempts to keep the tent from falling, that is Chinese nature; when he tries to rest from all this, that is his Indian nature. The races are interconnected; while we belong to one race, we also engage in the activities of other races. Each race, as God has granted a continent and land, has a specific atmosphere, weather, nature, and various animals and trees; all Muslims fast during Ramadan, the ninth month, as it signifies a shortcoming since nine is less than ten, and ten signifies perfection. Fasting prevents people from accepting anything less than perfect. Having an identity is important; a person without a name is like a house without an address; it receives no post, and without a name, it receives no mention and no resources directed towards it. Prophet Ismael (Ismaeel) is named thus as he was of mixed race, and his name means "difficult to name".

In modern Sudan, they intentionally marry strangers from other tribes and races to destroy tribal identity and race because they believe this will stop racism. This is the same group of people who used to have tribal scars on their faces to identify and show pride in their tribal and racial belonging. This is like saying cutting everyone's hand so they don't steal. The Quran says, "**If God wished, He would have made people into one nation**" (16:93).

The marriage of strangers leaves people without a sense of belonging to a tribe or race; they become what is referred to as mixed, leaving them without kings, lands, or dignity. This is why, traditionally, people refrained from marrying outside their tribe and race, simply because a child loses the ability to have a clear identity. Even if they are made to join their father's tribe and race, it makes them feel inferior for having less blood from them than other children of cousins who are fully blooded in their race and tribe.

Respecting people's identities and recognising that all identities have a right to exist and be respected, marrying strangers destroys identities and reduces belonging. The Quran says the devil claimed he would disfigure the creation of God. That clear sense of belonging is a beauty; confusion is not good. The human is not like a cow that eats directly from grass or a goat that sits under a tree's shade, but humans create homes and cook food; they need to have an identity to direct their deeds towards, to say, "so and so made this or that."

In America, interracial marriages were illegal, as they were considered akin to genocide and destroyed racial belonging. Modern America bans cousin marriage in many states.

Marriage of strangers was seen as evil and harmful, as it put or hid people of other tribes in the midst of a different tribe. They are seen as wolves in sheep's clothing, implying that they could be enemies of the tribe. It also decreases their numbers.

Speaking words against a race is considered racism, but destroying the race through mixed-race marriage is viewed as supporting the race when it's a mini genocide. Arabs call respectful strangers "amm" (uncle) to indicate they are safe and respected. Some then find this reason to marry strangers, calling them uncles and aunts.

Marriage to strangers leads to identity confusion. For example, it is like not knowing if a rope is really a rope or a snake; it's a worse state than if known to be a snake, as the fact it could be rope means they may slack from protection. The Quran says, "**They are confused, not knowing if they belong to this group or that.**" (4:143)

The benefits of racial belonging are having a body and blood from one tribe or race. This includes the ability to become royals easily, as they resemble their tribe and can then truly express and represent them. Additionally, they are most suited to the native land of their race; for example, a blonde person can camouflage in white snow and thus may not be easily visible to bears or, wolves, etc. If an Arab with brown skin, they can camouflage from snakes in the desert. Being from a tribe or race brings a person closer to understanding oneness, enabling them to comprehend a single God.

Parents should be asked for permission and blessing as children are given family names. For this reason, parental permission is part of the validity of marriage in Islam.

Prophet Muhammed said that in pre-Islamic times, they used to cast doubt on people's genealogy by claiming that some women married strangers, implying that all women engaged in adultery with stranger men.

Slave culture is becoming mainstream after the prohibition of slavery, where identity doesn't matter. So there is a lot of crime, such as a culture of prostitution, drugs and murder. This lack of identity in enslaved people has coincided with loads of stranger marriages where the child loses identity.

In Sudan, they question the humanity of people, seeing married life as a way of investigating and witnessing the humanity of people from other tribes and races. They say God commanded us to know people from other tribes and races. However, this is the role of royals and ambassadors. There are cultural centres and documentaries about different tribes and races.

Stranger marriages are used as a scientific analogy to explain cancer. Cancer is a very terrible disease that is difficult to cure, and a person cannot work, marry, or have children while undergoing the painful treatment. Arabs call it the "evil" disease. Prophet Muhammad (pbuh) referred to it as "namla" (ant) because an ant bite causes swelling. In cancer, the body starts creating different tissue in place of the original disease. Arabs saw marrying strangers from their tribes or races as bringing people different from the original. This decreases the function of the original tissue as resources are diverted to the new tissue.

Babies are born covered in blood, meaning they are born from a blood relation, which means cousin marriage.

Chapter 12

Ownership

This is a controversial topic. The idea of men owning their wives comes from the concept that she is related to him in marriage. It is not meant to offend or subjugate women; instead, it is a matter of responsibility, akin to a parent owning their child or a Royal owning their subjects. Owning each other can also be romantic, and many lovers say, "You are mine," expressing the greed of love.

Among Arabs, they believed that a man owned his cousin, and so even when she wanted to marry a stranger, she had to seek his permission. The basis for the man owning his cousin stems from the fact that she is similar to him. A man doesn't own all his cousins, only the ones most like him and most compatible with him. This girl is called Haleela in Arabic; the Quran states, "halail abnakum." The Quran uses halail, which is the plural of haleela. The Quran forbids a man from marrying the halail of his children. The Prophet

Muhammed (pbuh) stated, "Marry compatible women and marry your children to compatible people." The basis of a man owning their cousin is their similarities in flesh and blood. This is like if a ten-year-old boy cuts ten trees, a twenty-year-old man cuts twenty trees, and a thirty-year-old man cuts thirty trees. Then, they raised a dispute about how much each cut in trees. We will know how many each one cuts in trees, not only because of their standing next to them but also because of their capability that corresponds to their age. So, this similarity between tree cut and age is the basis of ownership. Likewise, the similarities between cousins are the basis of their ownership of each other. This similarity is not only in flesh and blood but also can be in similarities of parents' jobs, level of beauty, age, and marital status.

The world, due to containing purity such as rain and rivers, indicates that God owns it. Likewise, the cousin is like the girl in blood, flesh, and genealogy, so he owns her. The fact that the cousin owns his cousin and has preference over other men in her marriage means that taking other girls is akin to stealing. In Arab culture, when they wish to marry a girl to a man other than her cousin, he is asked for permission first as a way of being polite. Prophet Mohammed (peace be upon him) said marriage is like slavery, meaning ownership, which some Arabs call the marriage contract milka (the ownership). This implies that cousins are seen as being special and valuable. It is related that two women argued about who the mother of a baby was, so they went to the king. Prophet David, who was the king, said to the women he would divide the baby into half and give each woman a half. Hearing this, one screamed, and David said she was his birth mother. In cousin marriage, women find good meaning and no harm, so they deserve her more than others.

In David's judgement, lacking a cousin and marrying a stranger will cause the woman to be in hardship, like the mother of the baby.

In Islam, marrying enslaved people is a way of emphasising cousin marriage, where a man is said to own his cousin. If the enslaved person becomes the ownership of a man, she is like his cousin, and so he can marry her and have children with her, just like Prophet Muhammed (pbuh) married Maria the Coptic, who was enslaved. This wife is called "Malikat Yameen".

Men in Arabia are allowed to kill for their cousin, as she is considered property, and in Islam, people are permitted to kill to preserve ownership. Marriages between strangers assume God owns a boy or girl; they do not accept ownership of cousins. This view is widespread in the Middle East alongside the spread of politics such as Communism, where personal ownership is not encouraged.

When a girl marries a stranger, his family keeps telling her that they gave her a man and riches, but when he's a cousin, he's hers without anyone telling her they gave her something.

In the past, Arabs and Muslims would tell their sons from a young age that they have cousins so as not to become interested in strangers. Likewise, men meant to marry strangers are told they deserve the most beautiful. If a girl rejects him, they say he will find better than her. Stranger marriage is like a slave market where people find their worth based on who they end up marrying. How lucky they are is based on how much worth the marriage partner and in-laws appreciate them during the wedding and dowry presents.

Feeling needy in stranger marriages is humiliation. Marriage of cousins is pride and respect. They are asking for what is his, and to what is his he is more preferred to be given than others. Muslims should feel dignified and should not feel inferior.

Arabs insult a man as "*khawal*", meaning he does not benefit his own people. Prophet Muhammed (pbuh) said, "**The best of you are those good to their families, and I am your best, so my goodness is to my family**".

Some think that if they marry their cousin, they will be normal, but if they marry strangers, they will see them as important guests, spoil them, and treat them better than their cousins and family.

Men were helpful to women and children, providers and protectors, so they were considered deserved cousins, which is considered praiseworthy. Sexual desire is very painful and uncomfortable, so in His mercy, God allowed there to be cousins, and ownership shows compassion.

Chapter 13

A Real Marriage

Arabs traditionally consider cousin marriage to be a real marriage. This contrasts with the English word "marriage," which is derived from "more-age," as marriage happens after a child grows up, and "wedding" from "we-they-in." In Arabic, marriage is "Irs," from the words "Aar" and "Si." The word Arr means nakedness, and "Si" means wrong. The total meaning conveys that nakedness is wrong. They refer to the nakedness related to the genitalia and the sexual act from strangers; thus, strangers' marriage is deemed wrong. They believe that even cousins who are not married and are distant assume there is a problem, suggesting differences in genitalia and sexuality. When they marry, this erases any notion of their differences and highlights their similarities. Hence, cousin marriage and compatible unions are seen as pure, chaste, and devoid of sexual implications.

As a general rule, similar things are brought together while different things are placed apart. So, when similar cousins are distanced, each in their own home, this implies differences and is, therefore, shameful. However, when cousins marry and unite in one household, the notion of differences in genitalia is erased. This means marriage is pure and beneficial for both the couple and society.

People pour sugar into the sugar container and likewise with coffee and tea. When similar, there is no harm; the same applies to joining cousins who are similar and compatible. Arabs have a special term of insult for those not married properly. It is "Maras"; it is an insult to say one is not married properly, implying not married to a cousin. Girls are insulted as "Gahba," derived from the words "ga huba," which means to understand love and relationships with strangers.

Chapter 14

Humanity

Cousin marriages shows humanity. The fact that a child becomes exposed to the meanings of sex from a young age by parents who are strangers is sexual abuse. As humans, we should be kind and considerate and empathise with those in harm or pain, let alone commit injustices that harm people. The children of cousin marriage are born from the relationship with the uncle (un-kill); they are kind and against murder and harming others, so they represent the epitome of what is considered humanitarian and, therefore, human.

It is the case that a child from stranger parents suffers sexual abuse from their parents, who constantly describe sex as different and joined—the description of the act of sex where different genitalia are joined. This reminder of sex from childhood can reach hundreds of thousands and millions as they age, and thus, it is a suffering that no normal person can withstand. This raises doubts about the humanity of children of strangers, who are traditionally questioned in Arab culture, whether they could be demons. God says in the Quran, **"demons from the humans and demons from the spirits (jinn)"** (6:112). However, it is difficult to say that children of strangers are jinn (spirits who take human form) and not humans since they do not shape-shift like other jinn. Nevertheless, they are creatures of the unknown; God says, **"God creates some humans from what they don't know"** (16:8). This means they are outside the known cousin's marriage.

The devil in Arabic is called *Iblees* and is from three words *ab lays swa* (lit. Parents not similar), so this is the name of the head devil. He is named this since this is his job, to inspire people to marry strangers to bring children who are atheists, aware of sexual description from a young and without spirit and empathy and so can harm and kill others.

The parents who play with the act of sex in doing it with a stranger are playing with the act of life. This means that God could punish them by giving them life after death and become zombies. This is because they do not live life properly, and so they will not die a proper death, and their death is interrupted by states of life, making them zombies. In this way, they lose their human status. Prophet Muhammad (peace be upon him) said that when people pray to God for peace and blessings to his soul, God will give him life again in his grave, and he will return the prayer. He also said the Earth does not rot the body of the Prophets of God.

Chapter 15

The Nature of the Genitalia

Genitalia is in the middle of the body, and the middle is where two things meet. This makes it a place of creation since creation is about putting things together and joining them. God is pure and was not created, so He abases creation by classifying the genitalia as a place of exit for harm, such as faeces, urine, and farts. This emphasises the genitalia as a site of creation, where two legs meet and can also represent a place of harm. The merciful Creator created a reaction to it, to go deep inside the body as the female genitalia does or to protrude and extend further into the flesh as the male genitalia does. God created day and night to illustrate the differences between genders in the world. Therefore, in Islam, Friday, the sixth day, symbolises harm; since three lines create a triangle with sharp angles that can cause injury if touched, six represents double three, meaning excessive harm. This indicates that the sixth day suggests that night and day are distinct, impure and harmful, making it a day of purity. Thus, Muslims have special worship on Friday, and they consider it a day of celebration. Gender is appropriate in cousin marriage. The absence of harm in cousin marriage signifies that both the female and male are free from harm; hence, it is a heterosexual relationship. However, the idea of harm regarding a stranger makes the relationship resemble homosexuality, which involves the anus, which is deemed unclean. Girls in the desert seek men who embody true masculinity and propriety, as they assist them in survival, and this is why even girls are keen to marry cousins.

The genitalia are a response to the harmful and disgusting idea in it. This is by escaping, such as overcoming harm in male genitalia, the penis goes outwards, or in female genitalia go inwards, escaping the harm. Cousin marriage also has ideas of escaping harm, from the meaning of "further of the bother", so naturally, the genitalia support the idea of cousin marriage.

Genitalia is sensitive as if made for cousin marriage. This is because the cousin lacks harm as they are the father's brother (so further from the bother) relationship. When there is no harm, a person can touch the thing much, so the human genitalia, as it is intended for the cousin, has sensitive parts (penis glans and clitoris), meaning touch is interpreted as being much.

Traditionally, it was taught that cousins would have genitalia the size of each other. Different families, tribes, and races have different-sized genitalia, so the cousin was the best fit.

The Quran demands women not to be beautified in public as it reminds them of femininity and female genitalia. That is because women are aware of the absence of their genitalia and want to compensate for this absence by becoming beautified. This is why, traditionally, beauty is associated with females. However, the Quran has the story of the extremely handsome prophet Joseph (as). This suggests that men who have the presence of flesh in their genitalia (the penis) are beautiful ideas to encourage people to seek the grace of Heaven. Since women have an absence in their genitalia, the vagina, traditionally, women were seen as sowers of corruption. Therefore, Prophet Muhammad (pbuh) said, "**The majority of the people of the hellfire are women**" (Bukhari). This is also the reason why some men fear women; they see them as dangerous, as they might be inspired by the emptiness in their genitalia to do evil. Forcing women to be absent from public life is also a reminder of absence in their genitalia, so it is shameful and not acceptable in real Arab laws. The Quran commands the Prophet's wives to remain at home to become available for students of knowledge. Black African, Arab and Indian women were seen as beautiful due to their black skin. This is because black skin means absence, reminding of the absence in the female genitalia.

Some Arab and Muslim women, such as the women of Sudan, do not traditionally wear black as it is a colour of absence and a reflection of female genitalia. The little black dress is considered sexy in Western countries. White skin is seen as beautiful since it carries connotations of purity. Omar (raa) said, "White skin is half of beauty." This is because white is the colour of purity, and God is pure. The female genitalia are empty and so reminds us of missing sex in the human face. This means women are a sign of God. The Quran has a whole chapter called "women". The fact that women remind of God, the creator, is why women create babies inside their wombs.

After puberty, girls start to bleed from their vagina on a monthly basis, and this is called menstruation. Menstruation in women carries many meanings, including that only blood relatives may touch where the blood comes out. This implies that sexual union is desired, and a girl can become pregnant. It also signifies femininity, as it involves the shedding of blood, thus highlighting beauty in women. In the Quran, if a woman reaches menopause, she is not required to cover her hair, but it is better if she does. This is because she is no longer considered sexually desirable to men. In Islam, gambling is forbidden, and so experimenting and seeing luck in marrying. In other words, like choosing a watermelon, you buy it, and you don't know if it will be red or not, sweet or not. In Islam, it is not allowed to marry a stranger and say, "Let's see what happens"; rather, marry a cousin and know what they and her family are like and what to expect beforehand.

Females are more worthy of covering their genitalia as it is absent, and people feel shame about exposing poverty.

In the genitalia, there is a thick membrane (the hymen) that covers the entrance to the vagina; it is destroyed in the first act of sex. This is a sign of the existence of God since it is pure, as it stops the male from joining the female easily. The fact that the hymen bleeds is a sign that this should be done by a blood relative. It closes the vagina, so it is a purity to be born with and should be reserved for pure relationships. The hymen is pure in a place that is not pure, so it is destroyed. It is a weird thing; one would expect it to stop the harm and preserve the pure. In humans, pure hymen is destroyed and remains in harm.

Islam is strict when it comes to killing animals for food; there are laws and recommendations. This means the destruction of human flesh, such as the hymen, has to be inside the regulations of a correct marriage of cousins. Killing humans is a great sin in Islam, meaning there has to be care for human flesh. In medicine, where they use dead human bodies, there is a licence and laws governing human tissue, likewise in operations on living people. Therefore, likewise, the human flesh of the hymen should be respected. The hymen is special flesh; it carries meanings of purity, femininity and honour; it's not like a fingernail where it can be easily cut and thrown away.

Men need to be very erect and strong in body to destroy the hymen and penetrate the girl during first sex, so it's traditionally seen as pride in men, and since it gives great pleasure, it was seen as should be for the cousin.

People are very protective of themselves; some own guns, while others carry knives into the wild. Therefore, it's difficult for them to allow a strange man to destroy their flesh by marrying them to a girl with a hymen.

Genitalia, even though disgusting and harmful, bring forth goodness: the birth of a new life. Prophet Muhammed (pbuh) said, **"Love your lover without extremism, for they may become your enemy in the future, and hate your enemies without extremism, for they may become your lover in the future."** (Tirmizi). This means that, although genitalia is disgusting, we shouldn't hate it too much since from it comes goodness, such as new life.

The genitalia are hopeless since there is no change or break from the disgusting excretions. The cousin carries good meaning, so it is a break from the meaning of harm; strangers carry meanings of harm and are dangerous. Therefore, some people marry strangers to express ideas of lack of mercy for those who do wrong and are therefore harmful, like genitalia. The Quran says, **"Even after prophets despair, God's help comes"** (12:110). This teaches us to show mercy even to those criminals who people despair will not change for good. The Quran says, "**Don't despair from the mercy of God**" (39:53)

Since women in the middle have an empty vagina, some people may think women likewise are devoid of sexual desire while men have strong sexual desire. Prophet Mohammed (peace be upon him) said women have greater sexual desire, but it is masked by their shyness or sense of dignity and shame.

Arabs wear jalabiya since it has no emphasis on the waist or genitalia, which can be a source of harm. It provides good safety in the desert by avoiding injury. Wearing trousers in Europe emphasises gender and includes details at the waist near the genitalia. This is done as a way for a gentleman to say, "I am male, I am strong, I can help."

In Islam, God curses women who imitate men and men who imitate women. This explains that men and women become one, meaning the sexual act, which is an impurity. Sex is a sign of God and the cause of life, so it should not be considered a game and taken lightly. Prophet Muhammed (pbuh) said no hermaphrodite will enter heaven. This means they will be assigned a gender before entering heaven. In marriages to strangers, the ideas of harm make men like women and women like men. Some girls don't want to be girls by marrying their cousins but rather identify as male by marrying strangers. Prophet Muhammed (pbuh) said cursed are women who are masculine and men who are effeminate.

Chapter 16

The Best Sex

The fact that God created sexual desire, which can be intense and painful, He created in His mercy partners, male and female. Just as He created the urge to breathe and created air, hunger, food, thirst and water. God does not merely create sexual desire but has created families, tribes, and races to find someone suitable, especially cousins.

The nature of sex is that people want to unify to become one in body and soul. Similarity makes it easier to become one, but differences can never truly unify, regardless of any connection in their genitalia. Cousin lovemaking is considered to be the best sex, as shared meanings and similarities encourage their joining, making it full of pleasure. Arabs call women involved in stranger marriages "Momes," meaning "no touch," since their sexual encounters are not deemed proper. Even when they touch each other's bodies, their differences prevent them from genuinely appreciating one another's feelings.

When people value sex, marriage, and children as superior life experiences, everything else reduces in value, sometimes literally, such as milk, eggs, and groceries, and all commodities become cheap. Our expensive lives are because people don't get great pleasure from cousin sex and marriage, so they look for pleasure elsewhere in food and shopping, making traders increase their financial value.

The nature of sexual desire is that it's strong and painful, and they want to repeat many times, especially for men, so when she is a cousin, she doesn't repulse him after a few times, but a stranger who feels disgusted may not want to have sex many times. Modernly, there is so much divorce because of marriage to strangers, while traditionally, when people marry cousins, they don't divorce much.

The more the female is more feminine, and the man is more masculine, then the greater the sexual attraction and higher intensity of the desire and the greater the pleasure and orgasm. In cousin marriage, the good meanings are that the male is masculine and the female is feminine.

Cousin marriage is called "*muhsan*". In the Quran, it means to be protected or just and have no harm. It is also related to the word horse in Arabic, and Arabs call horses "khail", meaning "imagination", because they run fast and a person questions if they imagined it or if it is real. This is how cousin marriage is seen, as something without harm and so good it is unreal. If something is too good, people question if they are dreaming and are told to pinch themselves since harm is real due to its danger of death. So, when something is too good, such as a cousin marriage, it is considered unreal and like heaven even though they are in this world. Cousin pure marriages will be in heaven, so it's a pleasure fit even for paradise.

Arabs call talking about the genitalia, its functions and sex when unnecessary as *Bazi* while the opposite of denying that people talk about the genitalia and sex even with reason, such as to a doctor, is *Fahish*. The Prophet Muhammed (pbuh) was described as being neither *Fahish* nor *Bazi*. People should not be shy from learning and educating about sex, especially in a religious context.

The greater the sexual desire, the greater the pleasure, so being pure and innocent gives more pleasure; so, the child of cousins has the greater desire, while a child of strangers is not very interested and needs reminders such as music, drama and porn showing naked women and suggestive and sexually arousing material.

The Prophet Muhammed (pbuh) said women are married due to their beauty, richness, genealogy, and social status, but the best wife is the religious Muslim woman. This is because sex is a sign of God. Sex, as the joining of the male and female genitalia, is a mirror to the human face, which is a sign of God. The face shows the male nose and female mouth not joining, so the face is pure and a sign of a pure creator, who is God.

Masturbation is sex with oneself. The face has sex, so many scholars, such as Hanbali, believe masturbation is allowed in Islam. In Arabic, it is called *Umirah*, meaning mini cousin. As touching the self is like cousin sex since cousins have similar blood and flesh.

The marriage relationship is not just about body and genitalia; there is an emotional, psychological and spiritual meaning. All this adds to the pleasure of the sexual act. Marriages etiquette is people do not have sex with strangers and anybody but become limited to certain people such as cousins. Stranger marriages are random, like animals. The Prophet Muhammed (pbuh) said couples about to have sex shouldn't become like animals and penetrate but do foreplay first.

Swearing is using genitalia, excrement and sex to describe or express pain, harm and disappointment. This is proof that sex can be used in negative meaning so as not to be fooled by sex with strangers, meaning love and a good life. Sex involves the genitalia, a place of harm that can be used to mean insult, abuse, and humiliation. God says, "**God does not like public expressions of harm except those who have had injustice done to them**" (4:148).

Straight women see other women as not being attractive; they are soft and weak, but men are straight in body, not curvy or bendy and strong, and so are attractive. Straight men see other men as hairy and strong and hard and so do not give comfort like teddy and need and would appreciate softer women. At the end of sex, there's an experience of intense pleasure. The Prophet Mohammed (peace be upon him) called *Isilah* from a word meaning honey. Cousin marriage is beautiful and with great sexual pleasure; however, in modern life, there are many interesting pleasures. This includes sweet drinks, technology, holidays abroad, etc, so people don't consider cousin marriage important.

The lack of sex is a great insult to humanity. Arabs insult "*kus umak*", meaning "your mother's vagina". This is to say the only sex they will get in this life is coming out of their mother's vagina during birth. Another insult in humanity is raising the middle finger, and it is to mean they deserve the finger and not a human penis. Prophet Mohammed (peace be upon him) companion Abu Bakr (raa) said to disbelievers insisting on paganism to "suck on idols clitoris" since sexual insult is less punishment than killing them.

Those who marry strangers pleasure limited to body, but cousin marriage has many meanings and ideas there is mental and spiritual pleasure as well as body physical ones. Cousin marriage is enough pleasure in the desert, but with marriage to strangers, finds they don't have enough pleasure and are still looking for things to give pleasure in life.

The genitalia, as mentioned before, are a reaction to harm. The male overcomes the harm and escapes outwards, what is called the penis, while the female escapes inwards into the body, what is called the vagina. All these escapes from harm are similar to the meaning of the cousin, the father's brother or further of the brother. When a male sees female genitalia, his penis becomes erect and escapes further outward, becoming strong, as if to be more careful since women show overreactions to harm. The male penis then penetrates the vagina to reach the womb, which carries meanings of comfort, mercy, and pleasure. This avoidance of harm in sex emphasises the meaning of cousin marriage, making it most suitable to be between cousins.

Females enjoy sex as they have a hole in their genitalia, and the penis fills it, so they no longer have missing flesh. Men have a penis, so they have extra flash and want to give the hole. Prophet Mohammed (peace be upon him) described sex as charity.

Just like kids can know their mother compared to other women, likewise Arab men are attracted to their cousins more than to other women. In terms of comfort and rest, sexual desire is stronger with cousins, but strangers, fears of danger make it seem difficult.

Men are scared of sex with women for the first time, thinking, what if he has no erection and cannot penetrate the virgin? This is why marriage to a cousin is important, as it signifies kindness. Women are scared of sex with men for the first time, as they worry about being absent of genitalia, lacking flesh, and fearing the man's reaction. The rupture of the hymen and its bleeding raises fears for both genders, especially the girl.

Men prefer virgins because they don't want to share with other men, as it causes problems for them, and they have to worry all the time. He would worry about what would happen if he wanted her back, and women should be a source of comfort, not fear and possible harm from her former partner. This is important because a man is seen as owning his partner, which provides him relief by being exclusive to him alone. The Quran states that Prophet Muhammed (pbuh)'s wives are not allowed to remarry after his death out of respect for him.

When not married, Muslims should suppress sexual desire, as sex outside marriage is not permitted in Islam and is severely punished. When unmarried, girls should wear hijab; boys should lower their gaze and increase prayer since the Quran discourages immorality. Prophet Muhammed (pbuh) commanded fasting to reduce libido. The Quran states, "**those who protect their genitalia from fornication and adultery**" (23:5).

Chapter 17

Truth

There is an importance for the person to be considered real, especially children. This is because when a person is considered real, they are helped if needed. There is a danger that children of strangers are considered unreal. Simply, who could imagine the overwhelming pain of knowing that sex from a young age is real? Children of strangers are allowed to know the description of sex from the fact that their parents are different and become one in marriage; likewise, genitals are different and become one in sex. Who could imagine kids like that existing? Mixed-race people are a minority and so rare that they are not believed to exist.

Ages ago, they didn't know if strangers could give birth, as everyone married their cousins. Some people are surprised to learn that other races have genitalia or have sex at all.

Prophet Ishmael rode horses to show that he understood that some people think he is an imagination and not real, as he was of a mixed race. Prophet Muhammad (pbuh) said Ishmael rode horses because horses are referred to as imagination in Arabic because they are fast; a person may think they have imagined them and not been real. Reasons some people perform stranger marriages include wanting children who look different and not common, as when people stare, misinterpreting it at times as beauty.

God says in the Quran, **"the devil promised to change creations of God."** (4:119). One meaning is children who look strange and do not belong to a certain tribe or race. Producing mixed-race children is racist, as they claim they create them to improve on their own features, thus belittling one race and praising another. This is common when Africans marry Caucasians; they say they will gain light skin, which they believe makes them beautiful.

Arabs consider cousin marriage to produce real people whose logic and mental reasoning can explain their existence. However, children of strangers are not too real and might not exist. God says, **"Like a mirage considered by the thirsty as a water lake"** (24:39).

Cousin marriage is backed by God, so the children of cousins are the truth. Children of strangers are not supported by mind, sense, or God so that they could be an illusion or hallucination. Disbelievers are weak in the sight of God; they were killed in war by the throw of sand from Prophet Muhammed (pbuh). The Dajjal, who is the Antichrist, is said to be confronted by Jesus and will disappear and perish by melting into a pile of salt. God says in the Quran, **"Truth has come, and falsehood has perished, for falsehood is easy to perish"** (17:81). Girls marry men to understand what a man is, to comprehend better the Prophet Muhammed (pbuh), who was a man; he was a biologically male human.

CHAPTER 18

Family Bond

The strong family bond and general love for family members are greater than for strangers. The care and love people hold for family members, like fathers, brothers, uncles, and grandparents, mean that cousin relationships have a foundational connection that stranger couples must start from scratch.

As children play together, after puberty, they separate, and marriage is a way of reconnecting between cousins who became distant after puberty. Cousin marriage has the advantage of getting to know one's own people and understanding how women or men are within their tribe and race.

Arab girls want to ensure comfort for their cousins; they care about how they eat, do laundry, etc. She wants him to live well. Arab boys want to provide, protect, and give children to their cousins. Additionally, when married within the family, relatives are keener to help when something goes wrong, such as illness or death.

The family bond is based on the womb, which is a rounded muscle, indicating a need and is connected to the genitalia of harm, symbolising the absence of harm. This connotes mercy, comfort, and pleasure. Consequently, family members who share a womb are kind to each other. The penis embodies ideas of overcoming harm and can also signify mercy; families descended from one man show kindness to one another.

As humans are weak creations, people fear loss of life and injury, and family is merciful. Strangers don't share ideas of mercy and kindness as they don't share a womb. For this reason, strangers are perceived as dangerous with ideas of harm, which stresses the mind and prevents relaxation, making arousal for sex and ideas of union difficult. Strangers can generally be overwhelming, disgusting, or repulsive; for this reason, rape by strangers can be a very stressful ordeal.

One of God's names in Islam is Al Hanan, which signifies the kind love of family. People who wish to know their cousins better are called *haneen*. Henna is significant as it continues to give more and more colour when left for longer periods. Therefore, henna is used to symbolise family love, and in cultures where cousins marry, such as among Arabs and Pakistanis, henna is used in body art. Hanan embodies loving connections, particularly for those who do not forget past relationships and desire to reunite with those they once knew. It's a special type of love. This is the kind of love that cousins share, which makes them want to be together for life in a marriage bond. Puberty only occurs when a girl is safe and provided for, so cousins, uncles, and family deserve to have a girl in marriage. The father and cousin provide protection and a sense of safety for her to go through puberty. In medicine, it is said that if a girl is not comfortable, well-fed, and not traumatised or stressed, she will experience puberty. A girl is owned by her cousin, and he prefers her. Prophet Muhammed (pbuh) said, "**Being ungrateful to their family is the reason most women go to hell**" (Bukhari), so girls should marry their cousins to show gratitude to their family.

CHAPTER 19

Safety

Men are stronger in body than women, so women need to be careful when around men. Stranger men pose a greater danger than cousins who care and are gentle with women because they are family. Domestic violence, rape, and murder of spouses were traditionally seen as being perpetrated by strangers, while couples who are blood relatives have safer homes where women and children feel secure.

In Islam, wearing yellow clothes is forbidden because they carry meanings of harm, and the main reason for wearing clothes is to cover such harm.

In traditional Arab and Muslim homes, men and women are separated into different rooms or halls so they can be comfortable and safe. God creates the moustache that separates the male-looking nose from the female-looking mouth. Women are separated from men as they are stronger, and there is a risk of danger to women who are weaker; they could be beaten, raped, or killed, so for safety, they are separated. This separation also upholds chastity to prevent the mixing of genders and maintain purity, as God is pure.

Marriage is the way to life, so errors in it are dangerous, and people may misunderstand individuals who engage in such acts as threatening and may harm them. This is the basis of honour killing—that those who engage in wrongful sex or marriage are deemed dangerous and therefore eliminated by death.

Part of accepting the cousin is that she knows men like him. As she accepts her father, brothers, and grandfather, likewise she will accept her cousin as a husband. Also, as her cousin owns her, he won't let others destroy her, or other men touch her with harm. Women are safer marrying cousins since people treat their ownership more respectfully, while they are careless with other people's ownership.

Since cousin marriage is a relationship between the uncle and father's brother or further of bother, this means they can be aware of each other without harm or death. This is based on the uncle's idea of peace and goodness.

The Law of Zuma states that similarities are safe, and differences can lead to fights, wars, and death. The law of life is that people consider others like them safe and fear those different from them. There is a Hadith that Abu Bakr (raa) felt he drank, too, as the Prophet Muhammed (pbuh) drank. People fear killing others in fear they will also die due to similarities between them. In Sudanese Arabic, they call a stranger 'Zoal', meaning "do not harm".

Wisdom is when to say women are weak and not discriminate against them. In Islam, men are obliged to provide for women, so they inherit more. The rule should be if it is to advantage women when mentioning their weakness, then to say it, but if it's to insult them and belittle then it is not acceptable.

Prince marrying a commoner can be interpreted to say women are inferior and can be harmed. Prophet Muhammed (pbuh) said, "**Marry compatible**", and "**Women are the other half of men**".

As part of recognising safety, men give gifts and dowry to prove they will be gentle and kind to the girl, as girls fear men. In Islam, dowry is part of the validation of the marriage. Prophet Muhammed (pbuh) said, "**Less dowry is blessed**" (Al Sakhawi) since it means the man is mannered, and the girl is mature and does not fear her cousin much. Stranger marriages are dangerous, so they must give loads of money in dowry; therefore, they are not blessed.

Arab men wear turbans. Prophet Mohammed (pbuh) said, "**The turban is an Arab man's crown**"(Alzrgani). In Arabic, It is called an *Imma,* like the word uncle. Men wear it to say they are thinking about their cousin marriage so he's safe and kind to other women and that he believes in God. Women in Sudan wear the "*toab*" in public. It is a long sheet of fabric that they wrap around themselves, it is to the same meaning of turban, that they are chaster and support cousin marriage. This is because wrapping means joining, and fabric means hiding, so they mean the joining where sex is hidden, meaning the cousin marriage.

People hearing a woman has a caring husband can be a deterrent from bullying, abuse and violence against women. Pride to be worthy to have a partner for sex, provision, protection, and children is an honour. To be worthy of love that is at the heart of marriage is a complement and, therefore, a source of pride.

Women's safety and protection are very important, such as protecting the tongue from harm from teeth. The mouth, which is a hole, is feminine, so protecting the tongue in the mouth is seen as a symbol of protecting women. Protecting children can also be inferred from the dangling small flesh in the back of the throat, the Uvula.

In Arab and Muslim societies, people are judged socially by whom they choose to marry. Those who marry strangers are seen as being unsafe, while those who marry cousins are considered safer.

Arabs traditionally fear that exposing genitalia and touching genitalia during sex with a stranger can offend, potentially leading to hatred and violence. A special word for a prostitute is "Bagi," meaning a girl who stays in the presence of men and is not scared or careless about her safety.

Prophet Muhammed (pbuh) asked a newlywed, "**Is she a virgin to play games with?**" (Muslim). In cousin marriage, the meaning of safety allows for jokes, pranks, and games without being interpreted as harassment, bullying, or aggression. People are serious with strangers. In Sudan, some brides and grooms spit milk at each other during the wedding ceremony. A non-virgin is serious and is less likely to enjoy games.

CHAPTER 20

Afterlife

Animals in Islam don't live forever; they will be raised on the Day of Judgement and judged among them, and then God will turn them into dust. However, humans have spirit and will live forever in Heaven or Hell. The fact that children from strangers have little or no spirit makes their eternity doubtful. Arabs call their sons Khalid, which means "forever," because they are born from cousin marriages and have full spirit. Therefore, will live forever.

There are also ideas that those who engage in sexual relations, which is the way to life, by marrying strangers may be punished by God by having their lives played with, so they don't properly die and may gain life in the grave and become like zombies.

One man produces two sons, and they produce children who marry to bring the older man back. This new man has a high percentage of blood and DNA from the first man. This is akin to life after death and serves as proof supporting the possibility of life after death. It is also a mercy to the first man that, when he dies, he doesn't completely die, as some of his remains in the new man.

Chapter 21

Legitimacy of the Child

The child of cousins knows God, but the child of strangers cannot be associated with God who created them; how can they then be related to their parents?

In cousin marriage, a man has children who are his, but when the mother is a stranger, they also belong to a different race and tribe, and men like their children to be theirs alone. The Prophet Muhammed (pbuh) said God says, "**I don't like partners; whoever assigns a partner with God, God will leave them to that partner**" (Altabari).

The Prophet Muhammed (pbuh) said, "**Women give birth to people like their brothers and sisters.**" (Ibn Uday). Men want their children to be like their own family. When a woman marries only a cousin, there are more reasons to believe she will be faithful. A man will know his children are really his because she is not interested in strangers; likewise, his cousin knows he will be faithful because he is not interested in strangers.

The importance of identity for the child, and they must know their birth parents, tribe and race, is because then he can safeguard who feeds them, protect them, and give them knowledge of God.

When a cousin marries a stranger, his cousin becomes confused, as people assume he married his cousin. The child can't believe their mother is the stranger but wants the cousin to be their mother.

CHAPTER 22

Eternal Love

The Quran promises believers they will gain pure partners in heaven. Cousin marriages are pure, as they unite similar people in blood and flesh. This means that even people in this life who marry strangers when they enter heaven will be made to marry cousins. This means the cousin is the eternal partner, and so one may as well marry them in this world in preparation for heaven.

For all bad reasons, people who avoid and reject their cousins will be improved in heaven so that they may enter pure marriage. The Quran says, "**God removes all hatred from their hearts**" (15:47).

Cousins can't get enough of each other, so God created eternal life in heaven because people cannot get enough of their partners, family and loved ones.

In paradise, God accepts pure relationships only, so impure relations with strangers are not allowed in paradise since they promote sins such as atheism, paedophilia, homosexuality and prostitution.

CHAPTER 23

Soulmates

The soulmate is usually someone who is like you, understands you, knows you the most, is similar to you and loves you the most. Traditionally, Arabs considered the cousin to be this person.

When people are similar, they become friends and lovers and respect each other, so marriage between similarities is seen to be best, and cousins are the ideal. By knowing himself, the cousin also knows his cousin because they are similar in many ways. A soulmate is someone who knows how to feel like you on the inside, so cousins are soulmates.

Some men married to cousins don't want their cousin wives to hear about men who marry strangers so as not to belittle men in their opinion. Likewise, some girls don't want their cousin husbands to hear that some women marry strangers for the same reason.

CHAPTER 24

Convenience

In the past, families and relatives lived in the same area of a city or village, so the people available for marriage were inevitably cousins and relatives, and so they married. This is also why, with modern transport and international immigration, the world has become more accessible to people of other tribes and races, encouraging marriages between strangers.

The Quran says to the Prophet Muhammed (pbuh) to marry **"from those who migrated with you"** (33:50). Thus, the Prophet gave preference to cousins who were with him in the city of Medina before those who were back home in Mecca.

Chapter 25

Independence

A good reason for cousin marriage is being independent of people. That men don't need other strange men to provide for their women. This is a powerful reason for the modernity of many cousin marriages in Sudan. In Sudan, they say "gati gadahak" (cover your plate), which means that families should not need other people to know about their food and life requirements. Poor men may need other men, but rich men don't, so marriage between cousins is seen as a status symbol.

Men used to be offended by a strange man providing for their girl. It is seen as an analogy for homosexuality, to be given by strange men.

CHAPTER 26

Beautiful Wedding

When Arabs and Muslims marry cousins in Sudan, they usually perform a ceremony called Jirtig. In Sudan, it involves the bride wearing red, the colour of blood, to express that they are blood relatives and cousins. They also wear gold, especially a gold hat called "Jadla," since gold symbolises safety and protection from harm. Additionally, they wear red silk bracelets, as silk represents choices and red signifies blood or family. Prophet Muhammed (pbuh) said he saw Aisha in a dream in a piece of silk. They also use perfumes such as sandalwood powder on their heads. All of this conveys that expressing their cousinship and relatedness creates a beautiful wedding.

The bride and groom cover their heads with a sheet of fabric called Firka. This signifies that they are wrapped in a marriage of cousins, not exposed or explicit in a strangers' marriage. Prophet

Muhammed (pbuh) is reported to have covered himself, his daughter Fatimah (raa), his cousin Ali (raa), and his grandchildren Hassan and Hussain with a sheet of fabric. This is called the Hadith of Kisa. The bride and groom wear golden-coloured crescents on their heads. The moon, which gives light in the dark night, is seen as a symbol of generosity. The crescent, a small moon, means little giving, such as in charity, so it symbolises mercy. As cousins share family and are kind and merciful, they wear the crescent to proclaim they are cousins. Also, the crescent is a symbol of the religion of Islam.

In seeing the beautiful ceremony conducted for cousin marriages, girls are encouraged to say yes to their cousins when they propose marriage. Those who marry strangers usually wear Western clothing, such as a black suit for the groom and a white bridal dress for the bride. Interestingly, those who marry strangers do the cousin ceremony to confuse people and feel accepted by society, as no one objects to the ceremony.

People should say "mabrook" (bless) to the best marriage, which is that of cousins. To bless stranger marriages of strangers is to support atheism, paedophilia, homosexuality, and prostitution. The marriage ceremony conducted does not make strangers pure, just as slaughter in God's name does not purify pigs.

Henna symbolises family love, as the colour darkens as if the family keeps visiting again and again. Henna on the hand to support cousin marriage; some wear it red to signify blood relations. Sudanese wear black henna to imply absence, meaning sutra or sex is veiled and unknown in cousin relations. In Sudanese tradition, even males have henna applied for their weddings. It is nothing fancy like flowers, just a plain covering of hands and feet with henna.

In Sudan, Arabs have wedding songs that express the fact that it is a cousin marriage. Songs such as "the groom is walking to the girl from his tribe", "today the bride has been picked and taken from her family", and "it is a straight and beautiful wedding". Sudanese wedding songs include: "He has had henna done, and his mother is pleased, and the youth gathered in their home; today he is led to his uncle's daughter, for he is straight." Another song says, "It is a straight and pure wedding, and angels support and protect him by the power of God." In another song, they praise, "And that by being straight, it will be a step towards all success and health in life.". There is also a song called "Ya Ramaza" (lit, law, order or government). It goes thus: "This is my maternal cousin who I think a lot about. This is my paternal cousin who's love burns my blood (or who cares about me). Yeah yeah, the groom should be like this, come on it's the law". Then when they sing "the groom should be like this", the dancing bride points to her husband.

Sneezing in humans spreads water droplets, traditionally interpreted as spreading purity. This spread supports spreading news of cousin marriage since it is pure and reminds one of God. Because stranger unions spread impure ideas, they go against human nature. In Sudanese wedding tradition, the groom sprays perfume on the guests to say they spread good ideas, which is proof of a pure Creator, i.e. Allah, the God of Islam.

Some believe that if strangers participate in a cousin's wedding ceremony, it legitimises their marriage as strangers. However, the ceremony is like spices to food, not the main dish. This means the ceremony doesn't make marriages between strangers valid.

CHAPTER 27

Knowledge of death

Traditionally, marriage is seen as a rite of gaining maturity and becoming a proper adult. This is because, during the first sexual experience, the hymen is torn and bleeds, which provides a clue to death and indicates that the body will eventually be destroyed. The orgasm during sex, which leads to conception and life, also emphasises the importance of existence. All this leads the couple to become safety-conscious and, therefore, more protected in life from death. This, however, can only be the case when the couple comes from the same background, so the hymen can be a clue for both the man and woman. However, if the woman is a stranger to the man, her hymen doesn't inform him about his own flesh and body, only that of her people.

Since the hymen provides a clue to death and the destruction of human flesh after death, traditionally, in Arab law, girls were killed if they were found to be not virgins on their wedding night; it was seen as revenge. If a girl is not a virgin on her wedding night, her husband can stab and kill her because she didn't allow him to understand death and God. Arab and Muslim girls see their bodies as a trust, not their own, to be given only to their husbands. This is part of the chastity and honour of Arab and Muslim women.

When a person does not know death, they do not estimate it correctly, either thinking it's too easy or too hard, but destroying the hymen provides practical assistance in understanding death. Then, the couple knows and can overcome the fear of death and the destruction of their body in the grave after death. This is one reason for the importance of cousin marriage. Arabs who live in the desert are always keen to marry cousins and for early marriages to keep young people safe. The Prophet Muhammed (pbuh) said that knowing Aisha, his only virgin wife, "**is going to be his wife in heaven; it made death easy**" (Ibn Asakir).

People know that when facing death, they must be careful of themselves and others. They become kind and gentle, while those who do not understand death are unserious, careless and dangerous. Taking care of children and babies requires an awareness of the danger of death.

The bride is traditionally shy and serious-looking on her wedding day as she is a virgin and is about to have her hymen destroyed. Modern brides laugh and joke and are confident, as many, unfortunately, are no longer virgins.

When people understand death, they don't want to die, so they desire children who will survive them, allowing them to continue living in the world through their blood.

This is the reason children are seen as a mercy; they ease the pain of death for their parents and family; thus, they should be shown mercy and made to feel cherished and happy.

Traditionally, Arab men would fight for their cousins, and some even kill men who try to marry them. The destruction of the hymen is a symbol that whatever comes between them is destroyed, so it's very romantic.

When a man destroys the hymen of a stranger during the pleasure of sex, he associates their death with pleasure, which may lead to a liking for killing them and war. In Sudan, Arabs killed their son who refused to marry his cousin, usually by stabbing him in the stomach. One important reason is they feared he would marry a stranger and provoke war, so for the tribe's security, he was killed.

After a man knows death after destroying the hymen, then he is safe to travel and work, so he gains more money, etc. The Quran says, **"Marry the poor; God will enrich them"** (24:32). God will enrich them, as they mature and can do better work. Prophet Muhammed (pbuh) married his daughter Fatima to his cousin Ali when he was poor and only had his fighting shield. In virgin sex, there is human blood associated with the pleasure of orgasm. This can drive a man insane, leading him to kill his wife to see more blood or to kill her family and tribe if they are strangers, again seeking the pleasure of their blood.

There is a whole race of people called Africans who find life and death important. Even the way they look support that a person should not die. They have black skin, which covers flesh and veins to say exposing internal flesh leads to death. Their short, coarse hair, even in females, is to say death not good; since hair is devoid of feeling, and so is like a dead body. Prophet Muhammed (pbuh) said, **"mention death much"** (Tirmizi). The Quran says, **"Every soul shall taste death"** (3:185).

Chapter 28

Knowledge of Family

Marriage leads to knowledge about each other and the existence of the other gender and provides resources within the family. When a girl marries her cousin, she realises that men do indeed exist in her family, and the man becomes aware of the genuine existence of women in his family, too. This leads to a better understanding and respect.

A man who marries his cousin gains insight into women, thus becoming gentler with his sisters, mother, grandmother, and nieces, as he learns more about women from his wife's company. Those who marry strangers do not relate their experiences to their sisters and other female relatives because they are strangers, perhaps from a different tribe or race.

Some men marry cousins because they are accustomed to their own family, language and culture and do not desire what is different. They are set in their ways.

Chapter 29

Preserving Richness in the Family

Preserving richness in the family is the most common reason for cousin marriages in the developed world, for example, Pakistanis in the United Kingdom. They say they are trying to preserve wealth for family relatives. Prophet Muhammed (pbuh) said, "**The best among you are those who are good to their families, and I am the best; my good will go to my family.**"

The most common answer people give for why they marry cousins is that they want to preserve money within the family. This safeguarding of ownership, in that money will remain and be shared with the cousin, is seen as a valid reason for their choice of cousin marriage.

Since they are treated normally at home, but in strangers' homes, they are guests and feel special, some think marrying strangers brings more pleasure. Inheritance is within the family only in Islam, so there is more sharing between families, especially as gifts are encouraged as part of maintaining good family bonds. If a woman is married to her cousin and he inherits from their mutual grandparents, she has more rights than strangers to enjoy the inheritance with him.

Chapter 30

Self-Love

Men are strong, hardworking and can protect themselves, so they like themselves, which makes them feel they deserve a woman who is like them, emphasising how strongly they accept themselves. The cousin may sometimes even resemble the man in his facial features, which shows how he respects himself. In Arabic, the word for woman, "mara," is derived from the word "mira," meaning mirror. In other words, the woman should mirror her man, indicating that she should be like him, and this is best when she is his cousin.

Other people in society may judge a man who marries a stranger as not accepting himself. This is important as it indicates he won't self-harm and consequently won't harm others. Therefore, men who marry cousins are considered to be safer, as they accept themselves and thus would not harm others for fear of punishment to themselves.

Women likewise, when marrying their cousins, show acceptance of their family and express gratitude, providing their services and resources to their family.

Arab men like their wives to be like them in description to express their identity. Those who accept themselves will do good to protect it from the harm of punishment.

Marrying a cousin shows self-acceptance, indicating they are safe since they will not accept destruction, since they will not face punishment for wrongdoing. People who do not accept themselves see themselves as inferior and are ready to be destroyed and unrestrained; they will do wrong and don't care if they are punished and face destruction and death.

Many royals who view their race as good and enjoy luxury help people accept themselves and feel pride. Pride is a prerequisite for self-acceptance and for accepting one's language, culture, and religion. Arabs have preserved genealogies, some of which trace back to Adam, the father of humanity.

Traditionally, Arabs consider children from cousin marriages to be tough and invincible, as they are created without shortcomings. Thus, they accept themselves and do not do wrong, and therefore will not be destroyed and die.

Chapter 31

Peace

Peace is about preventing war, and cousin marriage is often viewed as peaceful, whereas marriage between strangers may lead to conflict. Marriage to strangers disrupts bloodlines and marrying outside the tribe or race results in children who do not possess the features of their tribe or race, which can be likened to genocide. This can spark tensions between tribes and races and may result in hatred, destruction, and wars. The act of the first sexual contact, where the hymen is destroyed and bleeds, can inspire murder. It was seen in a man who orgasms as he destroys the hymen; he then may associate pleasure with destroying the flesh of people and may enjoy it to want to kill people in her family, tribe or race. This, in turn, leads to fights, murder or wars.

The act of sex involves dirty and harmful genitalia; therefore, sharing it with a stranger may lead them to misunderstand it as hate and humiliation or even to interpret it as wanting a fight or war.

CHAPTER 32

Mercy

Marriage to cousins is seen as mercy. This is because, for virgins, the first-time sex hurts, and so it should be with cousins since they are family and kinder.

The first sex is very painful and uncomfortable. It is like the flesh is being separated. Some bleed from the hymen rupture, and others don't. It takes around three times of sex to penetrate the woman fully. She may need to push the man away because of the pain. The Quran says, "**Prophet Muhammed (pbuh) as sent to be a mercy to the world.**" (21:107). This means his encouragement and command to cousin marriage is part of this mercy.

Chapter 33

Family Business

The marriage of cousins is helping in family business; brothers who marry their children to each other preserve their business. Family gatherings are seen as opportunities to strengthen work relationships and exchange business ideas. Marrying cousins means inheritance can be preserved and need not be divided among brothers; instead, it can be left for their mutual grandchildren to inherit.

Royals usually marry cousins to preserve royal blood and keep the crown in the family. This is because people of royal blood typically have features such as beauty, mental strength, and strong bodies, and they want their children to inherit these traits.

The bloodlines of Prophet Muhammed (pbuh) and his relatives and companions are usually sought to be preserved and not diluted by the blood of strangers, preventing them from becoming extinct. When a child is the product of a cousin marriage, it is more likely for them to inherit the skills and talents of the family, thereby preserving their work from one generation to the next.

CHAPTER 34

Pride

Some tribes and certain bloodlines or races feel they are superior, so their men and women prefer their own people to strangers. This is especially true of royals, Prophet Muhammad (pbuh) bloodlines, or people from wealthy countries such as Britain, so they wish to marry their own kind.

When men choose whom to marry, they traditionally choose someone to give life to, someone with whom to share food, shelter, and protection. Because all girls deserve the benefits of marriage, when it's random, it can hurt those not chosen. However, in cousin marriages, the girls not chosen can understand, and no offence is caused to them. Cousin marriage is seen as kindness in society.

CHAPTER 35

Culture

Some dislike marrying strangers from other races because they prefer women who wear their traditional clothes or can cook traditional food. His cousin or a woman from his tribe or race is more likely to promote his culture than a woman who is a stranger from a different tribe or race.

Those who marry cousins preserve culture, such as food, music, dress, and religion.

Chapter 36

Love

Some are just naturally sexually and romantically attracted to cousins more than to other women. Just like there is a natural emotion towards a mother or father, some men develop feelings naturally towards their cousins. An example of this is "Laila's Madman," who is Gais son of Almulawah and he became crazy after he was not allowed to marry Laila, his first cousin.

Cousin marriage has good ideas and beautiful meanings, so their love can be accepted as true. However, strangers carry ideas of harm, danger, and hate, so attention is difficult to interpret as romantic love.

CHAPTER 37

Shame

Some men and women are too shy to share sex and genitalia with strangers. They are simply too proud for others to know they have a shortcoming regarding their genitalia. Some men, knowing that their genitalia frightens girls, feel uneasy about marrying a stranger but want a woman whom they can comfort easily, such as a cousin. Some girls consider the fact that their genitalia is an empty hole as being "nothing to give," and so prefer cousins since strangers may become offended by the girl's genitalia. They simply don't know how men will react to the reality of their genitalia. They think that, at least, just like their father, brother, or grandfather accepted them as girls, their cousin is more likely to accept them than strangers.

The fact that we live in a time when a lot of homosexuals girls think, what if the man they marry is homosexual and so will not like their genitalia? Girls may also be ashamed that they get their period, and men may be shy to fart in front of a woman who is a stranger.

Getting naked in the presence of strangers is difficult.

Some Arab men are not aroused by women or girls, not their cousins, mainly because they are too shy to expose genitalia and ideas of harm to strange women. Prophet Mohammed (peace be upon him) did not accept any of the women who offered themselves to him in "heba". When a woman offered herself to the Prophet, a companion accepted her marriage proposal while the Prophet remained silent in his refusal to marry her.

CHAPTER 38

Strengthen Family Ties

Marriage between cousins is seen as a way to strengthen family ties. To start with, the wedding celebration will bring the family physically together. As the girl's father visits, he finds his nephew there as well, so cousin marriages strengthen family bonds. Nowadays, people fear the opposite—that if cousins divorce, it may lead to the entire family breaking apart and causing hatred and strife. Some even use this as an excuse for not marrying a cousin. This is as extreme as calling for all people to have their hands cut off to avoid the risk of theft.

Islam teaches kindness to relatives, and the Prophet said, "**keeping good relations with family lengthens lifespan**" (Ibn Hajar Alasglani).

CHAPTER 39

Mutual Family Interests

Cousins may have similar lifestyles, hobbies, opinions, or personalities. They may also share a love for their mutual grandparents, which brings them closer together.

Chapter 40

Better the Devil You Know

Cousin marriage produces individuals already known to be good in body, mind and soul. While strangers, genetic diversity leads to new people with strange looks and even ideas. Like a farmer or horse breeder choosing to produce offspring similar to their previous good produce.

Girls who marry their cousins believe the cousin is like a father, grandfather, brother, or uncle—simply a man she has a good opinion of, as they raised her from birth. She doesn't want to try a random stranger.

Chapter 41

Surname

When parents are related, the child can take the father's name and genealogy without offending or belittling the mother's name or genealogy since they are the same. This is why, historically, genealogy usually states the father and rarely states who the mother is since the mother is usually related to the father.

In Western countries, women sometimes take the surname of their husbands, but this can be seen as cheating, making it seem as if it is a cousin marriage so as not to shock their kids and society.

Arab and Muslim girls prefer to marry their cousins to give their children their identity and surname.

Chapter 42

Music and Film

Cousin marriage is recommended socially in the form of music. Music, which is the beating of instruments such as drums, accompanies lyrics about love. It was traditionally considered that the music was meant to bring attention and warn against what was said in the lyrics. Prophet Muhammed (pbuh) commented on this irony or contradiction by saying, "**Singing grows hypocrisy in the hearer**" (Alshokani). This is the case since they were not preaching love for strangers but were warning against it; thus, their message was not straightforward. For this reason, singers were considered homosexuals and people who were not sexually straight.

In a Hadith, it is said that when Prophet Muhammed (pbuh) was young, before Islam, he was a shepherd herding sheep. Then, one day, he wanted to party with other young men and girls; however, on his way to such houses, he heard wedding music, so he sat to listen to their teachings on chastity and purity. Then he slept, and when he woke up, he found he did not need to go partying.

Art is important to teach emotions, symbolism, and meaning to the children of strangers who lack spirit.

Instruments, possibly from words "in is true are meant" for a person to realise that they do not mean what they say; they don't support love, flirting, and rape in public.

Listening to music makes people ponder the absurdity of love, which is ridiculous, impractical, and a thing of fiction and fairytales. So, they want solid and serious relationships with cousins and relatives.

Some people want to have a story for their marriage, to be entertaining like the movies and music, so they marry strangers.

Love stories in movies and fairytales do not depict married life and children. This is so people don't consider them serious relationships or imitate them.

Arabs used to appreciate poetry, placing it inside the house of God. The similar endings of words in poetry are seen as the end of the human; the genitalia are similar in blood and flesh, meaning cousins.

CHAPTER 43

Fashion

R oyals and prophets marry cousins, and some blindly imitate them, deeming it a luxury, cool or blessed.

CHAPTER 44

Disgust

As mentioned before, the human releases disgusting excrement, and so the human can be perceived as disgusting. The wife cooks food or eats together with the man, and some people are disgusted to eat from or with strangers. While the cousin wife is family, it is an extrapolation from mother's cooking.

CHAPTER 45

Power

To be included in a tribe or race means one can be protected by them or considered powerful among them. God says in the Quran, "**Their category who protect them.**" (85:13). That sense of belonging is important, and a child from cousins is a full member of a tribe or race and will thus receive their protection, resources, love, and respect.

Chapter 46

Beauty

Family, own tribe and race see a person as beautiful and attractive. Arabs say, "Monkeys, to their mothers, are as beautiful as deer.". Those who marry cousins know for sure, they look attractive to their spouse.

Chapter 47

Respect Mecca and Yemen

God's house is in the Middle West of Arabia since the genitalia is in the middle, and the West is where the sun sets, so together, they mean covered genitalia or absence of sex, making it a place of purity, which can be a sign of God in Islam. Mecca is surrounded by mountains, and mountains are the strong joining of rocks, and joining and touch is impure. The House of God being in a valley symbolises purity, since valley is empty without joined rocks. Pilgrims go to perform Hajj to prove the existence of God. This means covering the genitalia is a sign of being a godly person in Islam.

Yemen is the region in the southwest of Arabia. South signifies the idea of things meeting, just like in humans, where the genitalia is low, as in the South. West represents what is confirmed to be true, as it is where the sun goes down, and the sun is harmful, as its rays burn the skin; thus, west signifies without harm. This makes Yemen an important place where harmful ideas about genitalia are absent, encouraging cousin marriage, which fosters kind ideas.

Chapter 48

Prevent Fornication and Adultery

Fornication and adultery go against the order and social unit of the family. A child is born weak and needs parents; it is important to emphasise chastity and faithfulness to have true, stable parents.

Sex with a cousin is more fulfilling and pleasurable as it has better meanings, and so a person refuses sex with strangers as he considers them less pleasurable and not fulfilling. In this way, they are more faithful. This means cousin marriage protects paternity, purity and chastity.

Fornication and adultery are especially offensive to honourable descendants of the prophet, the angels, and to God.

CHAPTER 49

Respect Women and Men

In cousin marriages, men are not allowed to choose and say they want this girl and don't want that, which degrades women. Rejection or being not chosen is very painful for girls who are gentle creatures. Cousin marriage is accepting fate; however the cousin may be, her husband accepts her as his wife.

Cousin marriages and marriage of compatible characteristics emphasise the traits of man which honour both woman and man. Woman are called Mara in Arabic from mirror since she is supposed to be like the man.

Those who marry strangers belittle women; they believe women don't contribute to genealogy and belonging. Children are born believing their mother's genealogy doesn't matter and that children belong to man alone. The Prophet Muhammed (peace be upon him) had descendants through his daughter Fatima, proving that women's descendants and relations matter. Women inherit and give inheritance in Islam.

Traditionally, it was considered that homosexuality insults men, as they are perceived as receiving like women. This debases men and mocks women.

Prophet Muhammed (pbuh) said, "**God does not like those who want to experiment sexually and want to have a taste of this girl and that girl**" (Alsuti).

The idea that women are inferior to men comes from homosexual men who prefer other men and refuse women. Mohammed, peace be upon him, was heterosexual and said that women are the other half of men.

Men are strong; they help and give protection to their families. The Prophet Muhammad (peace be upon him) helped an old woman carry her heavy wood. This is why men in Arab culture are considered to deserve the praiseworthy meaning in cousin marriage.

Chapter 50

A Good Ending

It is the case that all people die; it is inevitable. However, we can choose how to reach that end. Everyone wants a good end to their life, which is called in Arabic Husn Al Khatima. We endeavour to live a good life; we worship God, are kind to people, give charity to the poor, visit the ill in the hospital, and try to be good people.

Cousin marriage is important in achieving a good end in that during the first act of sex, the hymen is broken, torn, and bleeds. This destruction of the hymen is a symbol of the destruction of the whole body after death. This act, therefore, provides evidence of death and the destruction of the body after death.

When a person destroys a hymen in a relationship of purity that emphasises the existence of God, such as a cousin marriage, it signifies they will have a good ending in which they will also acknowledge the existence of God. The Prophet Muhammed (pbuh) said, "**Whoever's last words are 'there is no god but Allah' will enter heaven**" (Alhakim). This indicates that a hymen destroyed in cousin marriage after a wedding that upholds all the pillars of an Islamic marriage signifies a premonition of a good ending in life. A hymen destroyed by a cousin is like a prayer for the end of life to be with family.

It is worth noting that a vulgar term for a prostitute in Arabic is "sharmoota" (literally evil death) since it refers to a woman who shows no respect for life and death, who plays with the act of sex—the way to give life—and has destroyed her hymen not with her cousin in a valid Islamic relationship. Prostitution is called "da'ara" (lit. leave it, it is explicit). This is because prostitution resembles a stranger's marriage; it is random, and the people involved are not blood relatives and do not share compatibility. This indicates it is a different joining, making it explicit in nature and describing sex as evil and forbidden by God, who forbids all fornication and adultery.

About the Author

Mysa Elsheikh is a Muslim Arab Queen (Um-fugara or Mother of the Poor) from Sudan. Her full name is Mysa, the daughter of Mohamed Elgasim and the son of Elsheikh Almagzoub. Mysa is the 61st direct descendant of Prophet Muhammed (pbuh) on her father's side and number 62 from her mother's side. She is also a descendant of Abdullah ibn Abbas (raa), Prophet Muhammed's cousin and a great Quran scholar. Mysa's parents are cousins twice over. Her mother's mother and her father's father are first paternal cousins, and her father's father and her mother's grandfather are first maternal cousins.

In May 2022, she married her first cousin to fulfil verse (33:50) of the Quran, after a dream of Prophet Muhammed (pbuh), Sheikh Hamza, son of Sheikh Awadallah, son of Elsheikh Almagzoub. On the 5th day of Ramadan 2022, I dreamt of Prophet Muhammed (pbuh) at the time my first cousin Hamza requested my hand in marriage. In the dream, I asked Prophet Muhammed (pbuh) "should I marry my poor first cousin, or a rich Arab stranger?" And the Prophet looked at me seriously and said, "I am Arab". I understood this to mean marrying my cousin because it is what Arabs traditionally did.

Mysa is a famous influencer in Sudan, and as of October 2024, she has nearly 100,000 followers across social media, with many viral videos watched by millions.

Mysa is fortunate to be a descendant of Prophet Muhammed (pbuh), and her genealogy to Prophet Muhammed (pbuh) is as follows:

Mysa, daughter of Sharif Mohammed Algasim, son of Sharif Magzoub, son of Sharifiya Sakeena, daughter of Sharif Fadul, is the son of Sharif Hussain, son of Sharif Ibrahim, son of Sharif Muhammed, son of Sharif Hamad, son of Sharif Muhammed Zumrawi, son of Sharif Muhammed Ahmed Al Bagir, son of Sharif Mahmoud, son of Sharif Hamad, son of Sharif Abdalkareem, son of Sharif Hassaballah Abu Khuf, son of Sharif Muhammed Almadani, son of Sharif Jabal, son of Sharif Abdullah, son of Sharif Barakat, son of Sharif Gasim, son of Sharif Rattib, son of Sharif Shahwan, son of Sharif Messaya, son of Sharif Taglab, son of Sharif Hober, son of Sharif Zakir, son of Sharif Sirajaldeen, son of Sharif Ja Alnaser, son of Sharif Gais, son of Sharif Shafi, son of Sharif Fayed, son of Sharif Umayra, son of Sharif Umran, son of Sharif Ali Noraldeen Ameel Murij, son of Sharif Hussain, son of Sharif Hassan Alakbar, son of Sharif Ali Albadri, son of Sharif Ibrahim, son of Sharif Muhammed, son of Sharif Abi Baker, son of Sharif Ismael, son of Sharif Umar, son of Sharif Ali, son of Sharif Usman, son of Sharif Hassan, son of Sharif Muhammed, son of Sharif Mosa, son of Sharif Yahya, son of Sharif Essa, son of Sharif Ali, son of Imam Muhammed Altagi, son of Imam Hassan Alaskari, son of Imam Muhammed Alhadi, son of Imam Muhammed Aljawad, son of Imam Ali Alrida, son of Imam Mosa Alkazim, son of Imam Jafer Alsadig, son of Imam Muhammed Albagir, son of Imam Ali Zain Alabdeen, son of Imam Hussain, son of Imam Ali, and son of Fatimah, daughter of Muhammed (pbuh), the Prophet of Islam.

www.ingramcontent.com/pod-product-compliance
Lightning Source LLC
Chambersburg PA
CBHW050358120526
44590CB00015B/1742